SENSE AND NONSENSE
ABOUT PRAYER

SENSE AND NONSENSE ABOUT PRAYER

By

Lehman Strauss

MOODY PRESS
CHICAGO

Printed in the United States of America

Contents

Preface

THE MESSAGE OF THIS BOOK speaks to my own generation. It grew out of a condition which has existed in the church as long as I can remember, and is growing increasingly worse. I refer to the low view of prayer. As I have traveled back and forth across our own nation and ministered in almost eleven hundred different churches, I have met professing Christians who admit to ineffectiveness in their prayer life.

Our loss of the biblical concept of prayer shows up critically at a time when we need it most. Religion seems to be making dramatic gains. But costly church buildings and programs which call for highly paid staff members are not sufficient in themselves to produce spiritual power. The alarming fact remains that while our gains are material, our losses are spiritual.

There are two major weaknesses, as I view the situation. *First,* there is weakness in the pulpit ministry. Too many congregations are not getting sound, solid Bible teaching. Biblical exposition is almost a lost art. Instead, topical sermons on social reform are the usual pattern. The *second* weakness—a prayerless church—grows out of the first.

One way to recover our spiritual losses is to return to God's Word. The decline of the knowledge and practice of prayer will then give way to a rediscovery of our lost spiritual resources. It is my humble opinion that a return to the biblical way of praying will bring spiritual power back to our lives and our churches.

May it please our Lord to use this small volume to assist believers in developing an effective prayer life.

A Personal Letter to My Reader

DEAR READER:

Thank you for picking up this little book. Frankly, I was a bit apprehensive about writing it. For a long time, two things restrained me from performing this task. First, I must confess that I *know* more about prayer than I have *experienced*. Second, there are those Christians who will never forgive me for making an unfavorable comment and offering constructive criticisms of the prayers people pray.

Then, too, it dawned upon me recently that those men and women in the Bible who were mighty prayer-warriors never read a book on prayer nor attended a seminar on prayer. They just prayed. But I could go to my library and take down any one of fifty books on prayer.

For almost half a century I have been listening to my own prayers and the prayers of others, and I am convinced that many of our prayers contain more nonsense than sense. Have you ever noticed the tendency of some Christians to go along with something as long as it is religious? The theology in the stanza of a hymn can be totally contrary to Scripture, but its defects are excused because it is a hymn. That it is poorly written and scripturally incorrect makes no difference. Or a sermon can be so poorly prepared and presented that it would embarrass even a deaf man, but still it will be excused by some because the pastor is sincere and well-meaning.

And oh, those public prayers! Some of them are said in a dead language fit for no environment except a cemetery.

9

But because they are prayers, the man is wrong who criticizes them. There are softheaded Christians who lose all common sense when they hear an *Our Father* and an *Amen*.

But shoddy stuff is shoddy stuff, whether you take it to church or leave it outside. A lousy song is still a lousy song, a lousy sermon is still a lousy sermon, and a lousy prayer is still a lousy prayer. (Note: Webster defines *lousy* as miserably poor or inferior.)

I received a real jolt after listening to a tape of a church service in which I had prayed and preached. The sermon was not one of my better ones, but it did make more sense than my prayer. After listening to what I said in my prayer, I asked myself, *Did I really say that?* But there it was, in my own voice. I could hardly believe my own ears. Since that experience, I have been paying closer attention to my own prayers and to the prayers of others.

In 1957, while I was pastor of a church in Detroit, one of our fine ladies said to me, "Pastor, I receive much help from your books. When are you going to write a book on prayer?"

"I'm not sure I can," I replied.

"Why not?" she insisted.

A bit reluctantly I told her I did not believe I had enough experiential knowledge about prayer to write a book. I had been studying the Scriptures for years and had read more than fifty books on the subject of prayer, but my writing would have been based more on head knowledge than on experience. Now, do not get the idea that I do not pray. As a matter of fact, I cannot recall a day in the past forty years when I did not pray. But I was not (and am not now) an authority in the art of praying. I have matriculated in the school of prayer, but I have not graduated. Nevertheless, I am venturing to write this book.

I do not expect that all of my readers will agree with me on every point I discuss. But just be patient with me, read all of the contents of the book, and then go back and prayerfully seek the mind of God. Remember, I told you that I am still a student in the school of prayer. If I waited to write this book until I had mastered the art of praying, the book would never be written.

Prayerfully yours in Christ,
Lehman Strauss

1

Sense or Nonsense?

HAVE YOU EVER LISTENED to yourself pray? Did it ever occur to you to think through and analyze your prayers, to examine precisely what you are saying? Do it sometime. Listen carefully the next time you or someone else is asked to pray. Then make notes. You might be convinced that those prayers did not make much of an impression on God.

Since 1963 I have been giving full time to an itinerant Bible conference ministry in churches, colleges, seminaries, and camps. I enjoy my work thoroughly, sometimes coming away spiritually refreshed in my own soul. But I returned from one conference that left me mighty low. It was attended by more than two thousand, including about three hundred ministers, at every service. All of the sessions were recorded on cassette tapes. I purchased the complete set of tapes, and frankly I find it hard to believe all that I am hearing.

For one thing, some of the prayers both amaze and amuse me. If some of the brethren who prayed were really talking to God, I cannot see how our heavenly Father could have been favorably impressed with their ability to hold an intelligent conversation. If one brother preaches the way he prayed, God pity his congregation. His words were dull, lifeless, at times theological and academic, but mostly incoherent. He sounded like a walking ghost. I thought to myself, *It must be a frustrating experience for God to listen to millions of prayers that say nothing, ask for nothing, and expect nothing.*

Right here, I am reminded of a story about an author who needed money and wired his publisher, "How much advance will you pay for my latest novel of fifty thousand words?"

The publisher wired back, "How important are the words?"

I like that! Some of the words that make up our prayers are not very important.

I must tell you about a good doctor who attended that conference to which I just referred. I met him for the first time over a cup of coffee between sessions. He seemed like a regular and normal kind of fellow. We returned to the auditorium for the next session, and as we entered the main hall, the chairman approached him, asking him to lead in prayer.

Well, he led all right, but to where, I will never be able to tell you. He had not uttered a dozen words before I was convinced that the man who had spoken to me at that coffee break was not the man who was praying. It was the sound of his voice that threw me off. He sounded as if he had developed a steeple in his throat, or as if he were talking through a stained-glass window. Now, I have never heard the voice of an angel, but he left me with the idea that he was trying to come through in angelic tones. It all sounded so unreal, so unlike the man himself.

Later that day, some of the boys gathered for a "rap" session. I stood on the fringe of the group and listened to a bit of — shall I say — *gossip*. The discussion was about the brother's prayer. One of the men said he felt it was wrong to criticize a minister's "public prayer voice." I called a moratorium on that one and quietly slipped out of the room.

During a series of Bible studies in a southern city, the host pastor called on a college professor to lead in prayer. The professor stood before the microphone, and what he said is here recorded, in part, word for word:

> God, You created the heaven and the earth, You created man, and You didn't do it by some evolutionary process. [*That bit of news must have been an eye-opener to God.*] And now, God, we thank You for sending the speaker. Bless the message of Dr. Strauss because we pray in his name. Amen.

Ah, brethren, that one touched my heart.

A tragic plane crash resulted in the death of all persons aboard. I was at a conference in northern Pennsylvania at the time. The conference director called on a man to pray. He apparently wanted to pray for the families who survived those who had died in the crash. Unable to recall the location of the crash, he said:

> Lord, bless that plane crash out there in — out there in — out there in — Well Lord, You know where it is; You must have read it in the morning newspaper.

Sense or nonsense?

While I was in Europe to minister to servicemen in the United States Armed Forces, several couples met for prayer in the apartment of a Christian officer. After we had been formally introduced and were seated, the leader began, "We have a special way of praying. No one is permitted to pray for more than one request at one time. If someone has forty-seven requests, he may pray forty-seven different times, but only one request at a time, please. And we don't say amen at the end of the prayer."

Come to your own conclusions about such restrictions people put on praying.

A pastor in a large city church invited me to conduct a Bible conference for one week, with sessions planned for both mornings and evenings. On Monday morning the service was well attended. Tuesday morning the attendance was about half that of the preceding day. Came Wednesday, and the crowd grew to a new high.

One young woman approached me with the question, "Did you miss some of us yesterday?"

"Yes," I replied, "the attendance was smaller than it was on Monday."

She proceeded to tell me why. "A group of us have our conversational prayer meeting every Tuesday morning."

I apologized for my ignorance and then asked what she meant by a "conversational prayer meeting."

"Oh, it's a new way of praying. God revealed it to ———."

"I am interested. Will you explain it to me?" I asked.

She paused and then said, "Well, it is not something I can explain. You would have to be there to experience it."

Now I have tried to be sincere in improving my prayer life, so I asked if she would arrange for such a meeting when I could attend.

Rather nervously she replied, "Oh no! That won't be possible. You see, when we meet for conversational prayer, it is for women only."

I might have been wrong in my conclusion, but somehow it just did not make sense to me. Since that experience, I have heard several different explanations of this "new" way of praying, but I cannot recall having read anything quite like it in the Bible. But I do have an open mind for the Lord to teach me. The desire to learn more about prayer is a growing one.

One of my favorite authors has written several books on prayer. In one of them, he has a chapter entitled, "Prayer Can Do Anything that God Can Do." Now that might sound good, but does it really make sense? Apart from our Lord Jesus Christ, there never has been a praying man, nor is there a praying man alive today who, through prayer, can do anything that God can do. There are things God has done, and can repeat, but He has not repeated them and possibly never will. Moreover, there are things God can do but which He will not do, notwithstanding our much praying. Still, there are Christians who have adopted as their favorite saying, "Prayer can do anything that God can do."

When I was pastor in Pennsylvania, I was called to the bedside of a dying man eighty-nine years old. His body was full of cancer. It was a family dream that he might live to be a hundred years of age. A daughter asked me if I would pray and ask God to raise up her father and spare him for eleven years more. I told her that I had no leading to make such a request.

Some bitter resentment showed as she snapped back, "Pastor, prayer can do anything God can do." In her expressed opinion, I was not a man of prayer. Yet, neither she nor the other members of that family could produce through prayer the result she expected of me.

In my opinion, she was misled by someone's nonsensical statement about prayer. Of course I believed that God was able to heal that old gentleman and keep him alive until he reached a hundred, but He did not do it. Nor did I have a sound reason to ask Him to do it.

Let Paul tell us why many of our prayers contain so little sense. He wrote, "We know not what we should pray for as we ought" (Ro 8:26).

Do you believe that statement? Will you admit that it is true in your own experience?

The text says that we have an "infirmity." The King James Version says *infirmities,* but the word is in the singular in the original, and should read *infirmity.*

In the midst of the turmoil, trials, and sufferings in this life, we are placed in a position of disadvantage which sometimes renders us ignorant when it comes time to pray. Under just such circumstances, Paul himself prayed ignorantly, three times, for the removal of his thorn in the flesh. But God had to say to him, "Paul, you are not praying right. You have asked me to do something I am not going to do."

Concerning this experience, Paul wrote:

And lest I should be exalted above measure through the abundance of the revelations, there was given to me a thorn in the flesh, the messenger of Satan to buffet me, lest I should be exalted above measure. For this thing I besought the Lord thrice, that it might depart from me. And he said unto me, My grace is sufficient for thee: for my strength is made perfect in weakness. Most gladly therefore will I rather glory in my infirmities, that the power of Christ may rest upon me (2 Co 12:7-9).

Romans 8:26 tells us that we all have a weakness when it comes to the matter of praying. Whether this weakness is in the thing we request, in the phrasing of the request, or in the motive, makes no difference. "We know not what we should pray for as we ought."

The heathen philosopher Diogenes gave this as a reason why men ought not to pray. But he was wrong! Instead of our ignorance silencing our prayers and leaving us in despair, we have the help we need in the person of the Holy Spirit, who serves in the role of advocate in our behalf. We do not know how to pray, but the Holy Spirit wants to teach us. Without Him, we Christians are powerless in our praying.

In the pages which follow, we will examine some Scriptures on the subject of prayer. I am particularly anxious to cover only those things which will instruct and edify God's children. If it is true that many mighty successes come to God's cause through prayer, then we should be willing to learn all we can about this important subject.

Recently I read again that passage on prayer in Luke 11. Our Lord had just finished praying to the Father. The disciples were close by, listening. No doubt they had watched and heard Him pray on other occasions. They knew the value and importance of prayer, so they came to Him with the request, "Lord, teach us to pray" (Lk 11:1).

The late Dr. G. Campbell Morgan emphasized the importance of their simple request. He suggested that we lose its meaning by adding to the disciples' words. They did not say,

"Lord, teach us *how* to pray." A great many people know *how* to pray, but they do not pray.

Lord, teach us to pray.

2

Prayer and Unconfessed Sin

IN MY TRAVELS, I usually try to read the church ads appearing in Saturday's newspaper. On one occasion, a minister announced as his sermon title, ''When Praying Is Sinful.''

I started to do some serious thinking about that topic. I asked myself the question, *Is it ever wrong to pray?* Now, I have no idea how that minister dealt with his subject, but I am convinced that there might be occasions when praying at least does not make sense.

It does not make sense to pray for anything if there is unconfessed sin in the heart.

> If I regard iniquity in my heart, the Lord will not hear me (Ps 66:18).

Sin unconfessed and unforgiven hinders prayer. Many a prayer bounces off the roof of the mouth, never rising any higher, for this reason. It is impossible for any Christian to experience a successful and fruitful prayer ministry if the sin question is not faced squarely.

This is not to suggest that God demands sinless perfection before He will answer our prayers. If that were the case, none of us would have our requests granted. But we do know that sin in a believer's life breaks that sweet fellowship between himself and God.

> He that covereth his sins shall not prosper: but whoso confesseth and forsaketh them shall have mercy (Pr 28:13).

Among the children of Israel, there were those who believed that God no longer answered prayer. They were saying, "He answered prayer in Elijah's day, but He isn't doing it now. His arm is no longer mighty; His ear has become dull of hearing." But the prophet Isaiah said,

> Behold, the LORD's hand is not shortened, that it cannot save; neither his ear heavy, that it cannot hear: But your iniquities have separated between you and your God, and your sins have hid his face from you, that he will not hear (Is 59:1-2).

The prophet was saying, "Don't blame God because He refuses to give you your requests. His power to save has not lessened; He is not losing His hearing. God never changes. He still wills that all men be saved, and His hearing is as keen as ever. He can hear the faintest cry of His weakest child. *You* are responsible for God's silence. The blame rests with you, not with God. Those sins you have not repented of have cut the lifeline of prayer. You raised the barrier between God and yourselves, and He will not answer you until you confess and forsake your sins."

Our churches could do with prophets like Isaiah, men who will tell it like it is, not fearing to expose sin. Not often do we hear men of God tell us that God hates worship and praying which are phony. It is brazen presumption which dares to ask anything of God while sin is in the heart. And if anyone feels I am putting it too strongly, then read the following verses:

> Bring no more vain oblations; incense is an abomination unto me; the new moons and sabbaths, the calling of assemblies, I cannot away with; it is iniquity, even the solemn meeting. Your new moons and your appointed feasts my soul hateth: they are a trouble unto me; I am weary to bear them. And when ye spread forth your hands, I will hide mine eyes from you: yea, when ye make many prayers, I will not hear: your hands are full of blood (Is 1:13-15).

Those are God's words, directed to His own people. Has

it ever occured to you that God hates sham in worship and prayers? That is right, God can and does hate. He tells His people they are wasting their time going through religious forms and ceremonies when their hearts are not right. He pays no attention to them.

There is, then, such a thing as sinful praying. If we refuse to judge and forsake our sins, we know that our prayers are an abomination to God. It is sheer nonsense to go on pretending, when all the while we have disqualified ourselves by refusing to meet God's requirements for successful praying.

And then Isaiah added the following exhortation from God:

> Wash you, make you clean; put away the evil of your doings from before mine eyes; cease to do evil (Is 1:16).

You should read the prayer Ezra prayed. One feature that stands out prominently is the confession of guilt and the genuine repentance. Get alone in a quiet place and read Ezra 9:6-15. Before you begin to read, search your heart before God and ask Him to speak to you personally. Then read quietly and meditatively. Read those verses more than once if you must, but read them until the message grips your soul. The opening words of that prayer will make one stop and think seriously. Ezra began,

> O my God, I am ashamed and blush to lift up my face to thee, my God: for our iniquities are increased over our head, and our trespass is grown up unto the heavens (Ezra 9:6).

Now, *there* is a prayer God will hear and answer. Ezra put himself on praying ground. He qualified himself to ask and receive.

Read the prayer Daniel prayed. It is much like Ezra's. What a searching prayer it is! That holy man of God said,

> And I prayed unto the Lord my God, and made my confession, and said . . . We have sinned, and have committed

iniquity, and have done wickedly, and have rebelled, even by departing from thy precepts and from thy judgments (Dan 9:4-5).

The apostle James wrote,

The effectual fervent prayer of a righteous man availeth much (Ja 5:16).

Our prayers can be earnest and heartfelt, yet never avail if there is unconfessed sin in us. We are not heard for our much zeal and fervor and emotion and agony. Praying when we are disobeying God is powerless praying. Let us never forget that right living is a necessary condition for the person who prays.

Can you imagine God forbidding a man to pray? Well, He did. He gave a clear command to Jeremiah not to pray for his own people. And God told Jeremiah that if he persisted in prayer, he would not be heard.

Therefore pray not thou for this people, neither lift up cry nor prayer for them, neither make intercession to me: for I will not hear thee (Jer 7:16).

By sins, I am not thinking only of those acts we put in the category of gross immorality. What about those sins of lying, wrath, stealing, corrupt communication, bitterness, evil speaking, and malice (Eph 4:25-31)? These are followed by fornication, uncleanness, coveteousness, filthiness, foolish talking, and jesting, "which are not convenient" (Eph 5:3-4). Some of these things we refer to as "little sins," but do not forget that it is "the little foxes that spoil the vines" (Song 2:15), and the "little member" that can spoil the membership (Ja 3:5).

The New Testament counterpart to the Old Testament exhortations to confess sins is in the first epistle of John:

If we confess our sins, he is faithful and just to forgive us our sins, and to cleanse us from all unrighteousness (1 Jn 1:9).

After David's disastrous fall into sin, he was cut off from fellowship with God. He had no liberty to pray or to worship God. He learned that it was useless to masquerade. So he came to God with an honest confession of his evil thoughts and deeds. And once again, David was in a position to pray. (Spend ten minutes in a quiet reading of Psalm 51.)

What God did for David, He wants to do for you and me, so why not go to God now, name that sin that has remained unconfessed, and start on the course that could revolutionize your prayer life. Let us search out and correct the causes of our prayer failures.

No one can both sin and pray. True prayer will prevent us from sinning, or sin will prevent us from praying. My own Christian experience is spotted by those occasions when I grieved God through sinning. Those were bad experiences which left a great deal to reflect upon. They were sad and disappointing times. But I am deeply grateful to my Lord for providing the means of restoration, whereby prayer could once more become effective.

It does make sense to confess our sins if we expect God to give us our requests.

> And whatsoever we ask, we receive of him, because we keep his commandments, and do those things that are pleasing in his sight (1 Jn 3:22).

3

Prayer and Selfishness

It does not make sense to pray with a selfish spirit.

Ye ask, and receive not, because ye ask amiss, that ye may consume it upon your lusts [pleasures] (Ja 4:3).

We are all naturally and basically selfish. Honesty must admit that even our prayers are selfish. It is possible that some of the good things we do are motivated by a selfish spirit. We will do well to examine our motives periodically, especially with regard to this matter of praying. James tells us that one reason for our spiritual poverty and powerlessness in prayer is a wrong motive. It is not necessarily the thing for which we are asking that is wrong, but rather the reason we ask for it.

A member in a church where I was pastor expressed a concern for the salvation of her husband. She had gone to several members of the church, asking them to pray for his salvation — a legitimate request supported by 1 Timothy 2:1-4.

One day I asked her why she wanted her husband to get saved.

She answered, "Because we would be so much happier in our married life. We could share the same interests, and life for me in the home would be much easier."

I am not critical of that woman for wanting those things. A home is doubly blessed when husband and wife walk together in the Lord. But to pray for her husband's salvation for the reasons she gave was selfishness on her part.

How different our prayer life would be if only we were genuinely unselfish! And when the Holy Spirit succeeds in teaching us this lesson, our prayer life will be free from a major hindrance.

Our Lord said,

> For where your treasure is, there will your heart be also (Mt 6:21).

If we are carnal and desire material things merely to gratify the desires of the flesh, we cut the lifeline of prayer. It seems from James 4:3 that those to whom James was writing might have placed more value on material things than on spiritual things. They were putting last things first and first things last, thereby preventing their prayers from being answered. To pray amiss means to pray with wrong intent. What folly it is to bother God for our desires, rather than asking for that which is His desire for us. The psalmist said,

> Delight thyself also in the LORD; and he shall give thee the desires of thine heart (Ps 37:4).

Now do not make the mistake of attaching the wrong meaning to that verse. It does not mean that God will give to us all those things we desire. I have thanked Him more than once for not giving to me every desire of my heart.

When my mother sustained an injury which resulted ultimately in her death, it was my desire that she would live. But apparently my desire was not God's desire. I did a lot of heart-searching then, discovering that my desire was for Mother's recovery first. But it was God's time to take her to Himself. My desire was natural, human, and therefore selfish. I failed to put God's desire first and mine last.

Now, as I look back on that experience, I can see my mistake. It was not wrong to desire life for my mother rather than death, but my motive was selfish, without any consideration for God's will. Therefore He did not give me that for which I prayed.

Have you ever tried to hide your selfish behavior behind a verse in the Bible? Many Christians do this, you know. Take, for example, Matthew 7:7, a frequently quoted prayer verse:

> Ask, and it shall be given you; seek, and ye shall find; knock, and it shall be opened unto you.

The majority of Christians will tell you that this is a verse that does not work for them. They are correct; however, there is a reason why it will not work. No verse in the Bible is intended to stand by itself — that is, it must be studied in its context. Now, if we fail to note that Matthew 7:7 follows Matthew 6:33, and that the two verses are contextually related, we can get into difficulty. Jesus had just said,

> But seek ye first the kingdom of God, and his righteousness; and all these things shall be added unto you (Mt 6:33).

If we obey the exhortation in Matthew 6:33, we will pray only for those things which concern God's kingdom and God's glory. The self-seeking person fails to put God's glory first; therefore when he asks, his request is not granted, and then he wants to charge God with not keeping His promise.

I am thinking of the man who came to Jesus with the request, "Master, speak to my brother, that he divide the inheritance with me" (Lk 12:13).

Now, there is a selfish spirit, if ever there was one. That fellow did not have God's glory at heart. He was a self-seeker; his request was a selfish one. The thing for which he asked could have been legitimate, but it was not motivated by a desire to glorify God. We know the man asked amiss, because Jesus did not grant him his request. Instead He rebuked the man when He replied,

> Take heed, and beware of coveteousness; for a man's life

consisteth not in the abundance of the things which he pos-
sesseth (Lk 12:15).

This man's request was motivated by a coveteous spirit.
The true purpose of prayer is not to obtain the things we
want from God but rather to make us content with the
things He wants us to have.

I know businessmen who have prayed that God would
make then successful and prosperous. A prayer like that
could be right or wrong, depending upon the person's motive. Suppose prosperity *should* come to a man who prays
for it. What will he do with the money after he gets it? Will
he honor the Lord in the disposition of it? Or will he spend
it on himself and his family for pleasure, luxuries and material goods? To pray from a heart that is set on things merely
to gratify the desire of the flesh, is senseless.

Check up on yourself the next time you ask God for
something. Examine the motive for that prayer request, and
see if you are seeking first the kingdom of God and His
righteousness. You might discover that you are asking
amiss. Surely, you do not want selfishness to rob you of
answers to your prayers.

A mother prayed amiss for her two sons — a prayer
Christ could not answer. Salome, the mother of James and
John, desired a place for both children in Christ's future
kingdom.

> Then came to him the mother of Zebedee's children with her
> sons, worshipping him, and desiring a certain thing of him.
> And he said unto her, What wilt thou? She saith unto him,
> Grant that these my two sons may sit, the one on thy right
> hand, and the other on the left, in thy kingdom (Mt
> 20:20-21).

No doubt Salome believed she had some warrant for her
petition. Moreover, she must have been sincere, because
she came "worshipping Him," but her request was denied.

Jesus said to her, "Ye know not what ye ask" (Mt 20:22). Let us be careful how we pray. Sincerity and a spirit of worship are insufficient to make up a valid petition.

And right here, self-examination is very important, lest we offer a prayer of pretense. The scribes and Pharisees were quite hypocritical in their prayers, but Jesus knew their hearts and motives. He pronounced a woe upon them for trying to fake it in their prayers. (See Mt 23:14; Mk 12:40; Lk 20:47).

It makes sense to examine our motives before we ask anything from God.

4

Prayer and the Holy Spirit

It does not make sense to pray if we do not pray in the Spirit.

> Praying always with all prayer and supplication in the Spirit (Eph 6:18).

Prayer and the Holy Spirit are vitally linked together. This is a truth taught in the Old Testament as well as in the New. Jehovah said to His prophet,

> And I will pour upon the house of David, and upon the inhabitants of Jerusalem, the [S]pirit of grace and of supplications (Zec 12:10).

I have spelled the word *Spirit* with a capital *S*, because I believe the reference is to the Holy Spirit. Possibly this verse has reference to the future outpouring of the Holy Spirit upon Israel. He is called the "Spirit of supplications" because it is He who awakens us to the desire and need to pray. He quickens the believer to pray now as He will in the day of Israel's spiritual awakening.

In the little epistle of Jude, we have an exhortation like that in Ephesians:

> But ye, beloved, building up yourselves on your most holy faith, praying in the Holy Ghost (Jude 20).

In these two phrases, "praying in the Spirit" and "praying in the Holy Ghost," we have one of the truly great secrets of prayer. If anyone were to ask me, what was the first great secret of a successful prayer life, I believe I would answer, "Praying in the Holy Spirit."

But what does it mean to pray in the Holy Spirit? The superhuman task of praying according to the will of God demands more than mere human reasoning. It needs the wisdom and power which only the Holy Spirit can supply. Human wisdom and human desires can achieve human results, but praying in the Spirit produces divine results. In praying in the Holy Spirit, the child of God has the power and wisdom of God to offset the power and wisdom of the world, the flesh, and the devil.

Real prayer is a spiritual warfare.

> For we wrestle not against flesh and blood, but against principalities, against powers, against the rulers of the darkness of this world, against spiritual wickedness in high places (Eph 6:12).

Here the praying Christian is between God on the one hand and the devil on the other. He is engaged in prayer warfare, and in his own strength he is no match for the enemy. Satan is a strong man, mightily armed (Mt 12:28-29), and only as we pray in the Spirit can we overcome him. The power to be victorious in prayer was promised by our Lord when He said,

> Behold, I give unto you power . . . over all the power of the enemy (Lk 10:19).

We Christians are in a conflict, and prayer is our mighty weapon. But we must view prayer not as a ritual but as a relationship with the Holy Spirit. The spiritual weakness that plagues most of us grows out of our failure to enter into that experience which Paul called "the communion of the

Holy Ghost'' (2 Co 13:14). Effective prayer is found only in the experiential knowledge of this blessed communion.

When we are praying in the Holy Spirit, we will not be trying to talk God into doing something He does not want to do, but rather we will be yielding to the Holy Spirit, who knows what is best for us. If we are not praying in the Spirit, we must be praying in the flesh. All spiritual prayers have their source in the Spirit. It does not make sense to pray if my prayers originate with me and not with the Spirit.

There are some things to remember if we are to pray in the Spirit:

1. There are times when we Christians do not know *how* to pray or for *what* we should pray.

> Likewise the Spirit also helpeth our infirmities: for we know not what we should pray for as we ought: but the Spirit itself [Himself] maketh intercession for us. . . . according to the will of God (Ro 8:26-27).

Here we are told that we have an infirmity which arises from our ignorance. We do not know what is best for us. It is right here that we need guidance, the guidance of the only Person who always and at all times prays "according to the will of God." The Holy Spirit assists us in our praying by giving to us the right desire and direction. Some of our prayers do not correspond to our needs. This is the infirmity that He "helpeth."

The word for *helpeth* occurs here and only one other time in the New Testament (Lk 10:40), where Martha requests help in the kitchen. What we need is the practical kind of help Martha was asking for.

2. We need to know and be aware of the fact that the Holy Spirit dwells in us.

> Know ye not that ye are the temple of God, and that the Spirit of God dwelleth in you? (Co 3:16).

There are some professing Christians who claim to be

saved but who say they have not yet received the Holy Spirit. If such persons have been saved, they have the Holy Spirit. It is not possible for one to be saved and not have the Holy Spirit.

> Now if any man have not the Spirit of Christ, he is none of His (Ro 8:9).

It will not be possible to enlist the Spirit's help in prayer if we do not have Him, or if we have Him and are not aware of His presence. It is common to hear someone pray, "Lord, send Thy Holy Spirit among us to bless us in this meeting." Such a request does not make sense. The Holy Spirit is here. Christian, He is in you. You can know Him and experience and enjoy His teaching and leading ministry. Do not treat this truth lightly. It is a mighty and holy truth to know. Your body is His temple (1 Co 3:16; 6:19-20). The more closely we associate our praying with the Holy Spirit, the better will be our praying.

3. To "pray in the Spirit," we must be careful that we do not grieve Him.

> And grieve not the holy Spirit of God (Eph 4:30).

How do we grieve the Holy Spirit? Look at the context of Ephesians 4:30. We grieve Him through lying, anger, stealing, dirty and useless conversation, malice, unkindness. These sins are repulsive to His holy nature and thus grieve and offend Him.

In all of our praying, we need the Holy Spirit's help. But if we have offended Him and our sins remain unconfessed and unforgiven, we cut ourselves off from the Spirit's help, which is necessary for effective praying.

4. In order to pray in the Spirit, we must be filled with the Spirit.

> And be not drunk with wine, wherein is excess; but be filled with the Spirit (Eph 5:18).

To be filled with the Spirit means to be controlled by the Spirit. When we are praying in the Spirit, the mind and the will are subjected to His control. "For as many as are led by the Spirit of God, they are the sons of God" (Ro 8:14), and in no area of our lives do we need His leading more than in prayer.

I am not a master in the important business of praying. The difficulties I encounter are so insurmountable that I need the great Teacher. At times the work of prayer becomes burdensome, and it is then that I am keenly aware that I must look to the Holy Spirit to seek His help. At other times prayer is a hard and bitter struggle, and my prayers are empty. Then I thank Him for His indwelling presence, I search my heart for any sin that might have caused Him grief, and I ask Him to take control of my prayers and my praying.

If we cultivate praying in the Spirit, it will bring about a change in our prayer life which we hardly thought possible. Prayer will no longer be a tedious and tiresome experience.

It does make sense to avail ourselves of the privilege of praying in the Spirit.

5

Prayer in Jesus' Name

It does not make sense to pray if we do not pray in Jesus' name.

> And whatsoever ye shall ask in my name, that will I do, that the Father may be glorified in the Son. If ye shall ask any thing in my name, I will do it (Jn 14:13-14).

> And in that day ye shall ask me nothing. Verily, verily, I say unto you, Whatsoever ye shall ask the Father in my name, he will give it you. Hitherto have ye asked nothing in my name: ask, and ye shall receive, that your joy may be full. At that day ye shall ask in my name: and I say not unto you, that I will pray the Father for you (Jn 16:23-24, 26).

"In my name" — what did our Lord mean when He told His disciples to pray in His name? Let me say at the outset that I believe prayer rises or falls with one's concept of Jesus Christ. The person who holds a light view of the Lord Jesus Christ cannot have a worthwhile prayer life. Jesus said,

> I am the way, the truth, and the life: no man cometh unto the Father, but by me (Jn 14:6).

This statement from Christ Himself is clear. That person who has never received Christ experientially and personally by faith can never find his way to God. He who rejects the Father's Son has no access to the Father.

More than once I have been in a strange city and needed to

ask directions. In one sentence, someone might tell me,
"Take the second road to the right, the fourth to the left, to
the traffic signal past the red-brick church, and you can't
miss it." But I would!

However, once I asked directions of a man sitting in a
pickup truck at a gas station. He said, "Follow me; I'll take
you there." To me, that man was the way, and I did not miss
it!

Our prayers cannot find their way to God except we come
to Him through Christ. Not everyone can claim the right to
come to God's throne of grace. The only persons who have
the right of access to God are those who recognize His Son.
Deny the Son, and we have denied the Father. Can any
person pray? The Bible does not say so! Prayer is
communion with God, and light can have no communion
with darkness (2 Co 6:14).

> For through Him [Jesus Christ] we both have access by one
> Spirit unto the Father (Eph 2:18).

I believe that many people find prayer a total failure
because they have not been born again. They do not know
that they have no rightful claim upon God until they become
His children. Jesus said to religious people who would not
accept Him, "Ye are of your father the devil" (Jn 8:44). Do
not think for one second that a child of the devil can claim an
answer to prayer, unless that prayer is a cry of repentance
and acceptance of Jesus Christ. If we are sons of God "by
faith in Christ Jesus" (Gal 3:26), we have the right of access
to God at any time, in any place.

What is meant by praying *in the name of Christ?* Certainly
it is more than a mere phrase at the close of our prayer — "I
pray in Jesus' name." I am not suggesting that to conclude
our prayer in Jesus' name is not included in our Lord's
statement. This is definitely what Jesus meant when He said,
"Whatsoever ye shall ask the Father *in my name,* he will
give it you" (Jn 16:23). This is the way I always end my

prayers, because the Bible tells me this is essential to getting my requests. For myself, I would not think of closing a prayer without saying, "in Jesus' name," or "in the name of the Lord Jesus Christ." While there is more than this involved in the words *in Jesus' name,* the words do mean just that, and I believe we are expected to follow that formula given by Christ Himself. Prayer in the name of Christ has power with God.

But I have an idea that many people pray "in Jesus' name," and still their prayer life is a failure. Why is this? Well, as we have noted earlier in our study, there are many requirements for successful praying. The absence of any one of them can hinder our prayers. Therefore it is not enough to pray merely *in Jesus' name.*

To pray in the name of Jesus is to pray for His glory, for His sake. That name represents the Person who bears it. Once I was asked to pray at a high school commencement. The principal asked me to write out the prayer and submit a typed copy to him for approval. When I questioned why he made such a request, he told me that the committee had voted unanimously to omit the name of Jesus so as not to offend the Jews who would be present. I told him that I could not pray to God and deliberately omit the name of Jesus Christ.

Praying that is not in the name of Christ is not in the Holy Spirit. Jesus said,

> Howbeit when he, the Spirit of truth is come. . . . He shall glorify me (Jn 16:13-14).

The rule of God's Word teaches me that I must pray according to God's way, not my own. To pray in Christ's name is to pray in union and communion with Christ Himself. It is not using His name as a magic formula to get what I want, but as a means of honoring and glorifying Him.

The prayer must be in keeping with the very nature and desire of Christ.

Prayer in the name of Jesus is an appeal to His authority. A sinner can come to God and receive salvation in that name (Mt 1:21; Ac 4:12; Ro 10:13). On the day of Pentecost, Peter exhorted the converts to be baptized "in the name of Jesus Christ" (Ac 2:38). Paul exhorted believers,

> And whatsoever ye do in word or deed, do all in the name of the Lord Jesus, giving thanks to God and the Father by him (Col 3:17).

The honor and glory of Christ's name are at stake in all of our behavior. We represent Him; we are identified with Him. So when we pray to God, we do so on the merits of His blessed Son.

One night when we were staying in a motel, there was quite a bit of disturbance. Someone on the outside was shouting and swearing. A man suspected that his wife was in one of the rooms with another man.

My telephone rang, and when I answered it, a male voice shouted, "If you have my wife in there, I'll kill you." Of course, his wife was not with me. The woman with me was my wife, who always travels with me.

A little later there was a loud knock on the door. I refused to open it, but I did call out, "Who are you and what do you want?"

A voice answered, "This is the police. Open in the name of the law."

If the policeman had given me his own name, I would not have opened the door. But when he came in the name of the law, I knew he had come with the authority of the city and state. I opened the door and introduced him to my wife. Satisfied, he and the angry husband went on their way.

The name of Jesus is the authority that opens the door into God's presence and gives us the right to be heard. Christ is not now here on earth to minister to His followers as He did to His disciples. But we can go to the Father, and when we do, it must be in Christ's name. God is not obliged to give audience to any person who does not regard and respect His Son. Anyone who does not honor and glorify Jesus Christ has no right to expect God to answer his prayers. One of the good things about trusting Christ and glorifying Him is that it puts us on praying ground, so that we may call upon God at any time. Prayer in the name of our Lord Jesus Christ prevails with God.

Many years ago I read an interesting story involving the late D. L. Moody. Mr. Moody was conducting a series of meetings in a town in Illinois. The wife of a well-known judge in that district came to Mr. Moody to ask him if he would please go to her unsaved husband and talk to him about his need of Christ. At first Mr. Moody was reluctant, because the judge was highly educated, while Mr. Moody was an uneducated shoe clerk. But he finally relented, agreeing to visit the judge in his private chamber.

Word had spread throughout the office that the young evangelist was coming to convert the judge. Now, the judge was a Unitarian and did not believe in the deity or the atonement of Christ. So when Mr. Moody entered the outer office, the clerk and stenographers giggled and made sport of him. They had discussed how quickly the clever judge would dispose of the young, ignorant preacher from Chicago.

Mr. Moody entered the judge's inner office, and the conversation was brief. He asked only that the judge would let him know if he were ever converted. Contemptuously, the judge promised that he would.

But within the year, the judge was saved. Mr. Moody heard about his conversion and went back to the town to visit him. He reminded the judge of his promise, and the judge gladly agreed to tell Moody about his conversion.

"One night, when my wife was at prayer meeting I began to grow very uneasy and miserable. I did not know what was the matter with me, but finally retired before my wife came home. I could not sleep all that night. I got up early, told my wife that I would eat no breakfast, and went down to the office. I told the clerks they could take a holiday, and shut myself up in the inner office. I kept growing more and more miserable, and finally I got down and asked God to forgive my sins, but I would not say 'for Jesus' sake,' for I was a Unitarian and I did not believe in the atonement. I kept praying 'God forgive my sins'; but no answer came. At last in desperation I cried, 'O God, for Christ's sake forgive my sins,' and found peace at once.''*

Now look closely at the following verse:

Having therefore, brethren, boldness to enter into the holiest by the blood of Jesus (Heb 10:19).

If this verse means anything, it means that only those persons can enter the presence of God who accept the teaching of the Bible concerning Christ's blood. To "enter into the holiest by the blood of Jesus" means that we can pray to God if we believe our sins have been atoned for by the blood of our Lord Jesus Christ. On the other hand, those persons who do not believe their sins are forgiven entirely on the ground of Christ's shed blood as an atonement, cannot really pray. A Unitarian might say prayers, but God must reject them. To all who reject the blood of Christ, real prayer is an impossibility. All persons who cut the blood of Christ from their theology and hymnology cut themselves off from approaching God in prayer.

It does make sense to pray the way our Lord taught us to pray, *in His name.*

I have decided to conclude this chapter with an excerpt from a prayer actually offered by a minister.

God, we come to You, God, asking You to send Your Spirit to this meeting, God. And God, we pray that You will bless the Word of God. We know, God, You can do this, God, for we pray in Your name. Amen.

* Reuben A. Torrey. *How to Pray* (Chicago: Moody, n.d.), pp. 47-48.

This prayer asked God to send His Spirit. That request does not make sense because the Holy Spirit was already there, indwelling every believer individually, and the entire body of Christ corporately. How much better and more accurate if the one praying had recognized the Holy Spirit's presence, thanked God for Him, and sought His leading for that meeting!

Now look at the last sentence in that prayer. "We know You can do this, God, for we pray in Your name."

Jesus said, "Whatsoever ye shall ask the Father *in my name*, he will give it you" (Jn 16:23). It is powerless and unprevailing praying that omits the name of our Lord Jesus Christ.

It makes sense to pray in Jesus' name.

6

Prayer and Faith

It does not make sense to pray without faith.

There are sincere people who have honest doubts about the efficacy of prayer. They have prayed sincerely and fervently, and for a noble cause, but their requests were not granted. One Christian showed me nine passages in the Bible where the Lord promises to answer prayer. The promises were direct and positive. And then he concluded by saying, "When I asked God to heal my wife, He didn't keep one of those promises. She died in the hospital." His prayer went up, but it did not bring anything down. At least, he thought it went up, but I have an idea it was grounded.

Prayer must be in faith. Unbelieving prayer is a waste of energy, time, and words. Our Christian life began with faith, and so it must continue by faith. As a dead man is no man at all, so a prayer without faith is no prayer at all. But the prayer of faith is God's delight. We are instructed,

> And all things, whatsoever ye shall ask in prayer, believing, ye shall receive (Mt 21:22).
>
> Have faith in God (Mk 11:22).
>
> Whatsoever is not of faith is sin (Ro 14:23).

Unbelief displeases God and must therefore be classified as sin.

> But without faith it is impossible to please him: for he that

cometh to God must believe that he is, and that he is a rewarder of them that diligently seek him (Heb 11:6).

George Müller left a lifelong record of his prayers and their answers — more than twenty-five thousand of them. On one occasion, when asked by a friend to explain his secret, Mr. Müller replied, "Have faith in God."

If I interpret George Müller correctly, he was not placing the emphasis on the word *faith*, but rather on the word *God*. George Müller knew God, so his faith was not in his own boldness and daring, but in the living God. It is the object of our prayers that makes the difference. "He that spared not his own Son, but delivered him up for us all, how shall he not with him also freely give us all things?" (Ro 8:32). To know God is to trust Him.

The faith that is essential to prayer is always faith in God. A person might have faith in a doctor, a bank, or an employer, but such faith is not faith in God. When we pray, we do not need confidence in ourselves nor in our prayers, but in God. There is a self-induced attitude of assurance and confidence that may be self-deception and not faith at all.

I call your attention to a remarkable scripture passage on faith and prayer.

> And this is the confidence that we have in him, that, if we ask any thing according to his will, he heareth us: And if we know that he hear us, whatsoever we ask, we know that we have the petitions that we desired of him (1 Jn 5:14-15).

"This is the confidence that we have in him." There is no point at all in coming to God in prayer if we do not have confidence in Him. "He that cometh to God must believe that he is, and that he is a rewarder of them that diligently seek him" (Heb 11:6). Faith is here declared to involve belief in a Person. Biblical doctrine is essential, but faith in God is more than faith in a creed. One can have no confidence in a God whom he holds in his mind to be untrustworthy. On the other hand, show me a Christian who believes God, and you have shown me a man of prayer.

Abraham had great confidence in God. Abraham and his wife, Sarah, were old, long past the age and stage of life to have children of their own. But one day God told him that he and Sarah would become parents of a baby boy. Moreover, God told him exactly when the child would be born (Gen 17:21). And when Abraham was one hundred years old, God kept His promise and Isaac was born (Gen 21:1-2). Fifteen hundred years later, the apostle Paul wrote of Abraham,

> And being not weak in faith, he considered not his own body now dead, when he was about an hundred years old, neither yet the deadness of Sarah's womb: He staggered not at the promise of God through unbelief; but was strong in faith, giving glory to God (Ro 4:19-20).

Abraham "staggered not" and was "not weak in faith" but was "strong in faith." Here was a man who had confidence in God. He did not merely believe *in* God, he believed *God*. When God gave the promise, Abraham put the amen to it. When we read that Abraham "believed the LORD" (Gen 15:6), we can translate it correctly that he "amened" God. When God told Abraham that He would give him innumerable seed, Abraham said, "Amen, Lord!" (So be it!). What confidence!

The epistle to the Hebrews spells out the definition of *faith:*

> Now faith is the substance [confidence] of things hoped for, the evidence [conviction] of things not seen (Heb 11:1).

Faith takes the promise of God, and says, "I am confident that it will be exactly as God said it will be, because I have confidence in God."

Beware of that nonsensical prayer meeting where emotions run high and where the excitement and frenzy are mistaken for great faith. I have been in some meetings like that. The late C. S. Lewis left us a good word on this in his *Letters to Malcolm: Chiefly on Prayer*. He said,

> We must not encourage in ourselves or others any tendency to work up a subjective state which, if we succeeded, we should describe as "faith," with the idea that this will somehow insure the granting of our prayer. We have probably all done this as children. But [that] state of mind . . . is not faith in the Christian sense. It is a feat of psychological gymnastics.*

My belief in the possibility of prayer is based upon the doctrine of God. Because I believe in God's ominscience, omnipotence, and faithfulness, I can depend on Him. Only the person who knows and trusts in God, and who has asked of Him and received, has proved the objective value of prayer. If you tell me God does not answer prayer, I will write you off as a person who either does not know God, or does not trust Him, or both. Discover the God of the Bible, place full confidence in Him, and then you will begin to learn how to ask and receive. While I cannot comprehend God fully, I know that He has perfect knowledge and unlimited power, and that He loves me and is concerned for my welfare; therefore I will trust Him.

James wrote,

> If any of you lack wisdom, let him ask of God, that giveth to all men liberally, and upbraideth not; and it shall be given him. But let him ask in faith, nothing wavering. For he that wavereth is like a wave of the sea driven with the wind and tossed. For let not that man think that he shall receive any thing of the Lord (Ja 1:5-7).

To waver is to doubt. If you have any doubts about God, why pray? Let not the person who has doubts that God can and will answer prayer, think that he shall receive anything

---

* C. S. Lewis. *Letters to Malcolm: Chiefly on Prayer* (New York: Harcourt. Brace & World. 1964). p. 60.

from the Lord. I believe it is at this point that some Christians go astray.

Early in my ministry there was a young woman in my congregation who expressed concern for her unsaved husband. She was saved shortly after their marriage, but her husband continued in unbelief. I asked her if she was praying for her husband's salvation, and she assured me that she prayed every day.

"Do you believe God will save him?" I continued.

This was her answer: "Not really. You see, no one in his family is saved, and he is so set in his ways."

Let not that woman think she shall receive anything of the Lord. Let us, as the apostles did, ask the Lord to increase our faith (Lk 17:5).

It does make sense to pray in faith.

7

Prayer and Unforgiveness

It does not make sense to pray with an unforgiving spirit.

I believe it is impossible for God to answer our prayers if we have an unforgiving spirit. To make requests of God while not forgiving others is sheer nonsense.

Is it possible that right here I am touching upon one of the most common causes of unanswered prayer? Listen to what our Lord Jesus Christ said:

> And when ye stand praying, forgive, if ye have ought against any: that your Father also which is in heaven may forgive you your trespasses. But if ye do not forgive, neither will your Father which is in heaven forgive your trespasses (Mk 11:25-26).

Here our Lord states distinctly that an unforgiving spirit makes it impossible for God to answer our prayers. In our day there have been a number of drastic changes made in methods and procedures in Christian work. These changes have caused much disagreement among Christians. I am thinking specifically of cooperative evangelism, the charismatic movement, and the like. These issues have resulted in splits in families, churches, and denominations. I personally have witnessed instances where professing Christians will not speak to one another. Bitterness and hatred linger in the heart. I know of one case where the innocent person is unwilling to forgive the man who wronged him. To date he

47

has been satisfied to go along with his own prayers unanswered for the carnal satisfaction of hating the man who offended him.

In the family of God we enjoy forgiveness, blessing, and answers to our prayers as we forgive others. The words of our Lord in Mark 11:25-26 are not addressed to unbelievers, but to Christ's own. We Christians cannot refuse to forgive anyone, no matter what the circumstances. When we do not forgive, we set up a roadblock in our prayer life.

> Lord, how oft shall my brother sin against me, and I forgive him? till seven times? Jesus saith unto him, I say not unto thee, Until seven times: but, Until seventy times seven (Mt 18:21-22).

Peter knew he ought to forgive the offending brother. He had learned this lesson earlier from the Lord. When Jesus taught His disciples the principles of prayer, He told them,

> For if ye forgive men their trespasses, your heavenly Father will also forgive you: But if ye forgive not men their trespasses, neither will your Father forgive your trespasses (Mt 6:14-15).

Peter was willing to forgive, but he figured that seven offenses committed by one brother was a lot to forgive. And seven being the perfect number, he considered himself quite spiritual if he forgave one man seven times. Quite frankly, I cannot see how keeping a record of the number of times a person has wronged me is a mark of spirituality. On the contrary, I rather look upon such behavior as an indication of spiritual immaturity.

We ought not to try to keep score of the number of times others have hurt us. God keeps accurate records, and vengeance belongs to Him (Deu 32:35). Let God take care of such matters. We should keep on forgiving, even to "seventy times seven," and by the time one reaches the count of 490 (if he must count), he should have gotten the victory over any bitterness and hatred.

The spirit of forgiveness should characterize every Christian.

> And be ye kind to one another, tenderhearted, forgiving one another, even as God for Christ's sake hath forgiven you (Eph 4:32).

God's full and free forgiveness to us should control our behavior in our relations with our fellowmen. This determines failure or success in prayer. God forgave us without any merit on our part; therefore we must forgive others, whether or not we think they merit it.

Look at those two little words *even as* (Eph 4:32), and you will see the perfect example of forgiveness. God forgave us for Christ's sake when we had wronged Him and did not deserve His forgiveness (Ro 5:8). So do not excuse your bitterness and unforgiving spirit on the ground that the one who has wronged you does not deserve your forgiveness. No one could ever wrong you as much as we have wronged God. Still He loves us and forgives. And now, "even as" He forgave us, so we must forgive others. We cannot be right with God when we are wrong with others.

A wealthy plantation-owner in Virginia had several slaves working for him. One day he discovered one of the slaves reading his Bible. He reproved the workman for neglecting his work and told him there was time enough on Sunday to read the Bible. He ordered the slave to be whipped and confined to a lock-up shed.

Later, passing by the shed, the owner heard a voice engaged in prayer. As he drew nearer and listened, he heard the godly black man beseeching God to forgive the injustice of his white master, touch his heart, save him, and make him a good Christian. Struck with guilt and remorse, the plantation owner turned to God in repentance and was saved.

In His teachings, our Lord brings us face to face with one big obstacle in our prayers — the sin of unforgiveness. Christians are weak, ineffective in service, and miserable because of this sin. And think of the misery other human beings suffer when we are guilty of this sin. When we violate God's law of forgiveness, a penalty is inflicted upon us, and others suffer with us. What every Christian owes to every other Christian is forgiveness. When we pray to the Lord, we have no right to expect His forgiveness and cleansing when we are unwilling to forgive others. Jesus said,

> Love your enemies, bless them that curse you, do good to them that hate you, and pray for them which despitefully use you, and persecute you (Mt 5:44).

A forgiving spirit is of prime importance if we are to have our prayers answered. And every Christian who does not have his prayers answered is a stumbling block to everyone within his circle of influence. We have no right to expect God to give us more than we are willing to give others.

Study Paul's prayer in 1 Corinthians 1:4-7, and you will see this truth in action. No church caused the apostle more concern and heartache than the church at Corinth. And yet Paul could say, "I thank my God always on your behalf" (1 Co 1:4).

Here is a practical lesson for us all. Paul did not begin this epistle with a rebuke or a criticism. He could have opened the letter by reminding the Corinthians of their many offenses. But here we see a beautiful example of a spiritual man. Their behavior had not been good, but Paul did not allow their bad conduct to diminish his love for them. He could write with a warm heart to his offenders, "I thank my God always on your behalf." That is the spirit which places the believer on praying ground.

Forgiveness was emphasized by our Lord when He gave to His disciples the principles of prayer. He taught them that the forgiveness of sins was a major problem of life, and that no man can stand on His platform of prayer who has not learned how to forgive as well as to be forgiven. He left no room for them to escape this fact.

And forgive us our sins; for we also forgive every one that is indebted to us (Lk 11:4).

He did not tell them that they could pray, "Lord, forgive me my trespasses and I will try to forgive those who have wronged me." He told them that when they had forgiven others, they could then claim their own forgiveness. And so we are trapped in an inescapable position: we cannot expect God to forgive us before we have forgiven those who have wronged us.

We must rid ourselves of all bitterness, hatred, and resentment if we want to be forgiven ourselves. We must forgive others, or we will never make any progress in prayer. Now, I know that nothing in all the world is harder for most of us than to forgive those persons who have really hurt us deeply. But forgiveness there must be, no matter how seriously we have been injured.

If your prayers are not being answered, search your heart, and see if there is not someone you have yet to forgive. See if you are holding a grudge against an individual, a family, or some Christian organization. If you are guilty, then you have an act of forgiveness you must perform. If you refuse to forgive, then do not bother to pray. You do not deserve an answer to your prayers.

It does make sense to forgive others before we pray.

8

Prayer and the Will of God

It does not make sense to pray if we do not pray in the will of God.

> And this is the confidence that we have in him, that, if we ask any thing according to his will, he heareth us (1 Jn 5:14).

The main thrust of this verse is in the words, *according to His will*. Praying according to God's will must of necessity bring to us far more contentment and happiness than if we could have everything we desired outside of His will. The will of God is described as "good, and acceptable, and perfect" (Ro 12:2), and that cannot be improved upon. I cannot imagine a Christian wanting anything less than that.

The psalmist said, "I delight to do thy will" (Ps 40:8), and "Teach me to do thy will" (Ps 143:10). And in no area of the Christian's life is the will of God more significant than in his prayers. To the degree that we lay the foundation for the will of God in our prayers, we shall enjoy it in all the experiences of life. Little wonder that our Lord taught His disciples to pray to the Father, "Thy will be done" (Mt 6:10).

The Father's will was at the heart of Christ's prayers. In a moment of great agony and suffering He prayed,

> O my Father, if it be possible, let this cup pass from me: nevertheless not as I will, but as thou wilt (Mt 26:39).

> O my Father, if this cup may not pass away from me, except I
> drink it, thy will be done (Mt 26:42).

On another occasion He said,

> I seek not mine own will, but the will of the Father which hath
> sent me (Jn 5:30).

Our Lord was always in touch with the Father, that He
might do the Father's will. The measure in which we Christians imitate our Lord in this will be the measure in which we
shall pray successfully. We have all thought at times that the
greatest happiness we can enjoy is to do our own will, but
that is wrong. How important, therefore, to learn to pray
according to God's will! And remember, then, it is the Lord's
will that we should have everything which will promote His
glory and our good. One obstacle to our complete happiness
lies within ourselves, in our wrong use of prayer.

I have not tried to list these prerequisites for sensible
praying in the order of their importance. If I were to do this, I
think I might put praying in the will of God somewhere near
the top of the list. I know that we must pray according to
God's will because the Bible says we must. Therefore we had
better learn how.

But can we know the will of God so that we might pray
according to His will? We certainly can. The big question
with most Christians is *how* to go about finding God's will in
the matter of prayer.

At this point, it should be said that there is not much sense
in praying for God's will unless we really want it. But someone will raise the question, "How can I say that I want God's
will if I don't know what it is?"

Ah, that is the big problem some of you have. You know
God's will is "good and acceptable and perfect" (Ro 12:2),
so why do you insist on knowing what it is before you pray
for it? You and I should want it and pray for it no matter what
it is. I have an idea that some Christians want to know God's
will about certain matters, not to obey it, but to see if it

coincides with their own desires. But that kind of inquiry after God's will is not honest. The Christian who wants to know God's will so that he might decide whether to accept or reject it is in serious trouble. That person knows nothing about praying in the will of God.

Let us be very careful that we do not deceive ourselves in this. I may *say* that I want God's will, but what I say might not be true. There are only two persons who actually know if I truly desire the will of the Lord — the Lord and I.

It is a common experience for me to be approached by young people asking how they might know the Lord's will for their lives. I have sometimes replied, "If God told you, even though you do not know now what it is, would you obey Him instantly?" You should have been close by to listen to some of the reactions and responses from these kids.

One seventeen-year-old fellow said, "How can I say yes if I don't know what it is?"

A girl, a nineteen-year-old college freshman, said, "That all depends." What she meant was that saying yes to God's will depended upon what His will was. She was not prepared to yield to anything or anyone, not even God, until she had compared His ideas with her own.

Frankly, I do not believe God discloses Himself to anyone who holds that kind of an attitude. Only the Christian whose will is surrendered to God can know His will. One of the purposes of prayer is to discover God's will in order that we might do it. There are Christians who shrink from making a full surrender to God because they are afraid God will ask them to do what they do not want to do. Those Christians know nothing of the meaning of prayer. The greatest prayer anyone can pray is, "Thy will be done."

Why should any person consider the will of God an unwelcome part of his Christian life? This attitude reflects an entirely wrong concept of both God and His will. God has a great purpose for each of His children, and they should welcome and embrace it as the most wonderful opportunity afforded them. The pleasure of God is not like the pleasure of man. God's pleasure is always profitable and good for His children. So before I pray, I must make certain that my request pleases Him. If I am asking for something that is not for His pleasure and glory, I may be certain that what I am requesting is not for my pleasure and profit. God's will for us is far more wonderful, more joyous, and more promising than anything we could design for ourselves. He has a much better life planned for us than we can possibly plan for ourselves. We should be ambitious to cultivate a healthy attitude toward the perfect will of God.

In my pursuit to become more skilled in knowing God's will, I am learning some lessons. For instance, the more we get to know God personally through the study of His Word, the better we shall be able to know His will. Many earnest Christians fail right here. They do not discipline themselves to read and study the Bible prayerfully every day; therefore they are confused about God's will, and their prayer life is a failure. The Christian who knows little about the Bible knows little about prayer. But I affirm without hesitation that those who will study the Scriptures prayerfully, trusting only the guidance of the Holy Spirit, will find new blessing and victory in prayer.

I remember reading about a mother whose baby was dying. Her pastor visited her and the child in the hospital in order that he might pray with her and comfort her. She said to her pastor, "O Pastor, please pray that God will heal my child and spare him to me."

The pastor said, "Are you sure it is God's will for your child to live?"

She replied, "I want him to live whether it is God's will or not."

The child did live. He grew to be a disobedient and unruly boy, and later a violater of the law. At twenty-one, he was sentenced to die for murder. How much better it would have

been for all persons involved had that mother known God's
Word, "We know not what we should pray for as we
ought. . . . We know that all things work together for good
to them that love God" (Ro 8:26, 28). Yes, there are some
things "we *know not*," one of them being how to pray. But
then, there are some things "we *know;*" we know that when
we leave the choice with God, "all things work together for
good to them that love God."

We can pray in the will of God only as we pray by the Word
of God. What the Holy Spirit teaches us through our Bible
study is inseparably tied to successful praying. The Holy
Spirit will never lead us to pray for anything contrary to the
written Word of God. There comes to my mind a passage in
the epistle of James:

> If any of you lack wisdom, let him ask of God, that giveth to
> all men liberally, and upbraideth not; and it shall be given him
> (Ja 1:5).

The entire letter in which this verse is found was addressed
to Christians who were suffering through a great trial. They
needed to know how to conduct themselves under that trial.
It is not easy to know what to do or say when one is passing
through a period of severe testing. Sometimes there is the
tendency to speak and act hastily; therefore wisdom is
needed. So what should we do? James tells us to "ask of
God. . . . in faith," and He will give it to us. It is never wrong
to ask God for wisdom. His wisdom is His will for our lives.

Paul prayed for Christians that they "might be filled with
the knowledge of his [God's] will in all wisdom and spiritual
understanding" (Col 1:9). To be without a knowledge of
God's will is to be like the captain of a ship lost at sea without
a chart or a compass. In God's Word, His will is revealed to
us. Without that knowledge, we fail in prayer.

It does make sense to pray according to God's will.

9

Prayer and Thanksgiving

It does not make sense to pray when we are not thankful.
Have you ever prayed with the feeling that your prayers
were not getting through to God? I have had that experience
more than once. But have you ever considered the fact that
ingratitude might be a hindrance in your prayers? It can be.

Prayer and thanksgiving are inseparably linked together in
the Bible. They cannot be disassociated. Give the following
verse a close and careful look:

> Be careful for nothing; but in everything by prayer and sup-
> plication with thanksgiving let your requests be made known
> unto God (Phil 4:6).

I once heard a ten-year-old girl try to quote this verse. She
began, ''Be thankful for nothing and anxious for everything.'' She stopped abruptly and said, ''That doesn't sound
right: I'd better start again.''

The girl's mistake illustrates a mistake too many Christians make — attempting to pray while ''thankful for nothing.'' Such praying goes into empty space and never reaches
God. After she had paused and reflected on Philippians 4:6,
the child quoted the verse accurately. Then I thought to myself, *If only we would pause and reflect on the many gifts
God in His grace has granted us, we could pray with a
greater measure of accuracy.*

The words *think* and *thank* come from a common root. If we would take the time to *think* more, we would undoubtedly *thank* more. We sometimes sing the song, "Count your blessings, name them one by one," but apparently we sing it as an exhortation to others — "Count *your* blessings" — when we ought to be counting our own. Prayer thrives best in the soil of a thankful heart. Some of the most wonderful seasons of prayer I have ever had have been times of praise and thanksgiving.

Look again at Philippians 4:6. Now underline those words, *prayer* and *with thanksgiving*. What a blessed combination! Whenever we approach God for anything, we should not fail to thank Him for those blessings and mercies we have already received from Him. Prayer without thanksgiving is ineffective.

It is my conviction that every time I come to God in prayer, my approach must be with praise and thanksgiving. It is a rude imposition to come to God asking for anything without saying thanks for past blessings. There should be that same urgency and definiteness in giving thanks to God as there is in asking of Him. It must be a grief to God to listen to requests from His ungrateful children.

God wants us to pray and make requests of Him, but He expects us to come with a grateful spirit. The devil does not want us to pray, but if we feel we must, he is satisfied if we go through the motions of praying, as long as we remain unthankful. No sin is too small to hinder prayer and turn praying itself into sin. Believe me, praise is essential to prayer. The psalmist wrote,

> Enter into his gates with thanksgiving, and into his courts with praise: be thankful unto him, and bless his name (Ps 100:4).

Read that one-hundredth psalm, and you will see that the dominating note is the obvious imperative of praising God and being thankful. Just as the right of approach to earthly monarchs is guarded, so is the right of approach to God. When we come near to the court of the King of kings, we must come with thanksgiving. If our hearts do not contain gratitude and praise to Him, the gate remains closed. The more we reflect on God's goodness to us, the greater our power in prayer. It is a solemn duty to consider the rich blessings and benefits we have received from Him. The recipients of God's blessings must be givers of thanks.

Many of the praise ballads in the Bible are prayers of gratitude to God. This is true of the prayer of Moses and the children of Israel after their deliverance from Egypt (Ex 15), and of the instruction to give thanks after they entered the promised land (Deu 26). Ezra thanked God for the gifts of King Artaxerxes, which helped to build and beautify the house of the Lord in Jerusalem (Ezra 7:27-28). The psalmist thanked God for creation (Ps 8), and for His greatness (Ps 96). Isaiah thanked God for the triumphs of his day as well as for the future triumphs of the coming kingdom age (Is 25). Jeremiah thanked the Lord for many evidences of divine goodness (Jer 32:16-25). Daniel kneeled down three times daily to give thanks to God (Dan 6:10).

A boy carrying a loaf of bread from the bakery to his house was stopped by his pastor. The minister said, "Charles, where did you get that loaf of bread?"

"From the baker," was the boy's reply.

"Yes, I know that, but where did the baker get it?"

"He made it," said the boy.

"But how did he make it?"

The boy answered, "Sir, he made it with flour."

"Tell me, where did he get his flour?"

"He ground it from the grain."

"Do you know where he got his grain?"

"Yes sir, he got the grain from the farmer."

The minister said, "Now Charles, I will ask you one more question, and I want you to think carefully before you answer. How did the farmer get his grain?"

The lad hesitated and then replied, "God made the grain grow."

That was exactly what the boy's pastor had hoped he would say. "You are right, Charles. Then, you got your loaf of bread from God. So remember, when you sit down to supper tonight, to thank God for it."

Have we forgotten that behind every good gift there is the divine Giver? My friend, you and I are dependent upon God; and when we fail to acknowledge this, we are denied the right to pray.

I received a rich blessing while reading the prayers of the Lord Jesus, noting the frequency with which He gave thanks.

> At that time Jesus answered and said, I thank thee, O Father, Lord of heaven and earth (Mt 11:25).

> And he took the cup, and gave thanks (Mt 26:27).

> And he took the seven loaves, and gave thanks (Mk 8:6).

> Then they took away the stone from the place where the dead was laid. And Jesus lifted up his eyes, and said, Father, I thank thee that thou hast heard me (Jn 11:41).

As we examine the epistles of Paul for their prayer content, we will find much thanksgiving.

> First, I thank my God through Jesus Christ for you all (Ro 1:8).

> I thank my God always on your behalf (1 Co 1:4).

> Wherefore I also, after I heard of your faith in the Lord Jesus, and love unto all the saints, cease not to give thanks for you, making mention of you in my prayers (Eph 1:15-16).

> Giving thanks always for all things unto God and the Father in the name of our Lord Jesus Christ (Eph 5:20).

> I thank my God upon every remembrance of you (Phil 1:3).

> We give thanks to God and the Father of our Lord Jesus
> Christ, praying always for you (Col 1:3).

> We give thanks to God always for you all, making mention of
> you in our prayers (1 Th 1:2).

> For what thanks can we render to God again for you (1 Th
> 3:9).

> Pray without ceasing. In every thing give thanks: for this is
> the will of God in Christ Jesus concerning you (1 Th 5:17-18).

> We are bound to thank God always for you, brethren (2 Th
> 1:3).

> But we are bound to give thanks always to God for you (2 Th
> 2:13).

> I thank God, whom I serve from my forefathers with pure
> conscience, that without ceasing I have remembrance of thee
> in my prayers night and day (2 Ti 1:3).

Whenever Paul prayed or spoke about prayer, he seldom
omitted the note of thanksgiving. This is why I am not
surprised at that which took place in the heart and home of
the Philippian jailer. Paul and Silas had fallen into the hands
of wicked men who beat and bound them. Their first response was to turn to God in praise and thanksgiving. They
did not question why nor ask God to set them free. Luke
says,

> And at midnight Paul and Silas prayed, and sang praises unto
> God: and the prisoners heard them (Ac 16:25).

Prayer and praise! There is that blessed combination
again. Things were not going smoothly for them when they
sang and praised the Lord. Those men were suffering hard-
ship. Yes, it is possible to be "sorrowful, yet always rejoic-
ing" (2 Co 6:10). We are not told what Paul and Silas prayed
about, but I will venture a guess that they prayed for the
salvation of their persecutors and fellow prisoners. Their
prayers and songs of praise were heard, not only by guards

and prisoners, but by God. That night, salvation came to a man and his household (Ac 16:30-34). The combination of praise and prayer produced results.

Thanking God is an essential exercise of godliness in which Christians should engage themselves at all times and under all conditions. When we omit thanksgiving from our prayers, we rob God of an honor due Him, and we render our prayers powerless. There are some ways in which we cannot recompence God; however, the gratitude of our hearts does please Him. When we remember God's goodness and acknowledge what He has done for us in the past, we open the door into His presence. If we will increase our hearts of this wonderful truth, our prayers will not be in vain.

> By him therefore let us offer the sacrifice of praise to God continually, that is, the fruit of our lips giving thanks to his name (Heb 13:15).

Christians who are mighty in prayer are those given to thanking and praising God. Try it!

It does make sense to include thanksgiving in our prayers.

10

Prayer and Abiding

It does not make sense to pray if we are not abiding in Christ and His Word is not abiding in us.

> If ye abide in me, and my words abide in you, ye shall ask what ye will, and it shall be done unto you (Jn 15:7).

If prayer is a mystery to you, it might be that here is the key that will unlock the door to a full and joyful life. There is in those words of our Lord a conditional promise to which the average Christian is a stranger. The number of petitions that have been denied us is more than we can count. There has been a reason for this. Either we have failed to meet the condition, or else God has failed to keep His promise. I am not prepared to charge God with failure, as I have heard some people do.

The simple condition in Christ's statement is that we abide in Him and His words abide in us. The striking conclusion in that statement is that we can ask what we will, and it shall be given to us.

The condition is in two parts. First, our Lord said, "You must abide in me." The word *abide* (Gr. *meno*) means to remain, continue, dwell, stay put.

Every saved person is said to be "in Christ," an expression Paul used not less than seventy times to describe the believer's new position. This new position becomes a fact at the time of salvation, establishing union with Christ. The baptism in the Holy Spirit (1 Co 12:13) seals the union experientially, so that the newborn child of God has been "baptized into Jesus Christ" (Ro 6:3). This new position of union with Christ is an unalterable one,

> For we are members of his body, of his flesh, and of his bones (Eph 5:30).

Right here we must note the difference between *union* and *communion*. The *union* is positional and unchanging; the *communion* is practical and can vary. In 1927 I was united to Jesus Christ, a blessed *union* that has continued unbroken to this very hour. But I cannot boast that my *communion* has been unbroken during those years. I have been "in Christ" positionally, a vital relationship from which I can never be separated (Ro 8:38-39), but there have been those times when I did not continue, remain, or abide in fellowship with Him. The relationship has never been severed, but the fellowship has.

Abiding always refers to fellowship, and only those persons who are saved are capable of this fellowship. The branch must first be in the Vine in order to abide in it. When the union takes place, the Vine and branches share a common life, the branches always depending upon the Vine. Therefore it is conclusive that no unsaved person can pray to the living God. The branch must be in the Vine and abiding in the Vine if prayer requests are to be granted. Those to whom Jesus addressed His words in John 15 were exclusively believers, Judas having already gone out.

I am not suggesting that there is a Christian who has lived every moment of his life in Christ in sweet, unmarred fellowship with his Lord. That would suggest sinless perfection in thought, word, and deed — a goal that none of us can attain in this life. The Bible tells us that in many things we all fail (Ja 3:2). But what I do see in Christ's statement is that when our communion is cut off, so is the pipeline of prayer.

But let us examine Christ's statement in the general context of John 15. He likened the relationship between Himself and His disciples to a vine and its branches (vv. 4-5), saying, "I am the vine, ye are the branches" (v. 5). Some branches bear no fruit, others bear fruit, still others bear "more fruit" (v. 2), and still others bear "much fruit" (v. 5). What makes the difference in the quantities of fruit?

When I was a boy, I spent part of several summers with an aunt and uncle in Florin, Pennsylvania. On their front lawn was a large cherry tree. I used to head straight for that tree upon my arrival, when the season was early and the fruit not fully ripe. I enjoyed that tree in spite of the stomach pains I suffered later.

I recall one branch on that tree that never did bear fruit. Every year that branch was there, continuing in union with the tree, but without fruit. There was a reason for that. None of the branches had life in themselves, but were dependent upon the sap, or life, flowing into them from the tree. Their fruit was the outcome of that life. For some reason, there was no flow of sap into that fruitless branch. Something hindered it from drawing the power necessary to bear fruit. Organically, it was a part of the tree, but it was not being nourished on the life-producing power of the tree.

Every Christian is in union with Christ, but not all Christians feed on Christ daily. And when the branch does not get its nourishment from the Vine, it is not abiding, and the branch that does not abide is fruitless and powerless in prayer.

When we look at the second part of our Lord's condition for asking and receiving our petitions, we learn how we feed on Him for the necessary nourishment. Jesus continued, "And My words abide in you."

Here again we see the relation between prevailing prayer and the Word of God. The Bible is the Christian's prayer book. When we neglect the daily, quiet, meditative reading of God's Word, we block the lifeline to God's throne of

grace. Our abiding in Christ through the Word is a life process that must never cease. Jesus said,

> I am the living bread which came down from heaven; if any
> man eat of this bread, he shall live for ever: and the bread that
> I will give is my flesh, which I will give for the life of the
> world. The Jews therefore strove among themselves, saying,
> How can this man give us his flesh to eat? Then Jesus said
> unto them. . . . He that eateth my flesh, and drinketh my
> blood, dwelleth [abideth] in me, and I in him (Jn 6:51-53, 56).

I think we have all asked the same question those Jews
asked, "How can this man give us his flesh to eat?" Jesus
answered that question for them and for us when He said,

> The flesh profiteth nothing: the words that I speak unto you,
> they are spirit, and they are life (Jn 6:63).

There we have Christ's secret to the abiding life, "If my
words abide in you." When the Word of God is controlling
the prayer life, "Ye shall ask what ye will, and it shall be
done unto you."

When the branch is being nourished from the life of the
vine, it will produce precisely as the vine determines. As the
vine produces fruit, the branches produce fruit.

So it is with prayer. If we are abiding in Christ through His
Word abiding in us, we will have no love but His love, no joy
but His joy, no peace but His peace, no desire but His desire,
no petition but His petition, no fruit but His fruit. Failure to
abide is one reason why prayers are not answered. God will
never fail to keep His promise, but we must meet the condition.

It seems strange that more importance is placed upon
prayer than upon Bible study. Both are important and necessary, but is prayer more important than the study of God's
Word? My own experience teaches me that what God says to
me is infinitely more important than anything I could say to
Him. Were it not for the instruction God gives me in His

Word, I would not know how to pray or for what to pray.

Fifteen men gathered to pray after the evening service during a summer conference. Some of the prayers were spiritually refreshing. But one brother prayed, "Lord, help us to read Thy Word more."

Now, that request just did not make sense. He was asking God to do something that only he could do. Did he expect the Lord to put a Bible in his hands, open it up, and cause him to read the words? It was possible for him to answer that prayer himself. Frankly, I felt he might have been better off had he gone directly to his room and spent the time reading his Bible.

A word of caution is necessary at this point. Do not think that because you read a chapter or two from the Bible every day that God's Word is abiding in you. I know a woman who boasted that she read the Bible through every year, but I would not consider her to be a spiritual person nor one who could prevail in prayer. The mere reading of the Bible per se will not produce power in prayer. The Word must be implanted in the heart, meditated upon, and obeyed. It is then, and only then, that our prayers are formed in accordance with the will of God. It is easy to deceive ourselves in this. The apostle James says,

> Be ye doers of the word, and not hearers only, deceiving your own selves (Ja 1:22).

At the risk of being labeled a heretic, I will knock out the props from under a false theory about prayer and its relation to spirituality. I have become weary of listening to preachers confuse people by telling them that if only they will pray more, they will become spiritual. The Bible refutes that dream. We do not pray to become spiritual, nor do we become spiritual by the saying of many prayers.

When we pray the Bible way, it is because we are already spiritual. Only a spiritual Christian prays the way he ought to pray. And true spirituality can be arrived at only as God's

Word is obeyed. The obedient Christian is the abiding Christian, and the abiding Christian enjoys an effective prayer life.

There have been times when I asked God for certain things which were denied me. But at no time did God fail to keep His promise. When my requests were not granted, it was because my heart was not occupied with Christ, and my thoughts and desires were not regulated by the Word of God. The longer I live, the more I learn that "Man shall not live by bread alone, but by every word that proceedeth out of the mouth of God" (Mt 4:4). When I am in fellowship with my Lord, and controlled within by His Word, I may have power in prayer. Every Christian who expects his requests to be granted must remember to obey the rule of *abiding*.

It does make sense to abide in Christ and have His Word abiding in us.

11

Prayer and Giving

It does not make sense for a stingy Christian to ask anything of God.

> Whoso stoppeth his ears at the cry of the poor, he also shall cry himself, but shall not be heard (Pr 21:13).

In that one verse of Scripture, you have a basic rule for successful praying. And yet, I will venture to guess that it is one of the least known of God's requirements for prevailing prayer. It is not a new prayer rule handed down recently by God, but an ancient one that has been bypassed for centuries by the majority of believers. And it is easy to see the reason why—it touches our money and earthly possessions. But there it is, like it or not.

God is the Patron of the poor. He said,

> He that hath pity upon the poor lendeth unto the LORD; and that which he hath given will he pay him again (Pr 19:17).

Those of us who are better provided for are expected to show compassion for the needy. God keeps records of our deeds, so we shall in no wise lose our reward if we share what we have with others.

But if we stop our ears to the cry of the needy, in due time we shall cry to God, but He will not grant our request. This is especially so when those in need are fellow believers in Christ.

I have been blessed recently through reading some of the prayers of Old Testament saints, many of whom are outstanding in history. Some of those spiritual giants experienced mighty victories in their own individual prayer lives.

Abraham is a remarkable example of the power of prevailing prayer. Have you read recently his intercessory prayer for Sodom, recorded in Genesis 18? It is a spiritual classic. The record begins with the statement, "Abraham drew near" (18:23), confessing that he was as "dust and ashes" (18:27), thereby expressing his deep humility of spirit. Once in the presence of God, Abraham began his intercessory prayer.

He prayed, "Wilt thou also destroy the righteous with the wicked?" (18:23). And then, with a clear and definite aim in his request and asking nothing for himself, he interceded for the righteous souls of that wicked city. He prevailed upon God to spare the city for the sake of fifty righteous people, then forty-five, then forty, thirty, twenty, and finally ten. Knowing that there were at least ten righteous persons, Abraham left off praying, having received assurance from God that his prayer had been heard and his request granted.

I cannot disconnect that prayer of Abraham from an incident recorded in Genesis 13. When the herdsmen of Abraham and Lot quarreled over whose cattle should graze where, Abraham said to Lot,

> Let there be no strife, I pray thee, between me and thee, and between my herdmen and thy herdmen; for we be brethren. Is not the whole land before thee? separate thyself, I pray thee, from me: if thou wilt take the left hand, then I will go to the right; or if thou depart to the right hand, then I will go to the left (Gen 13:8-9).

There was nothing mean or stingy about Abraham; he was a generous man. He did not leave the choice with Lot, but with God. His generous spirit was rewarded by God with positive answers to his prayers. We are reminded that such was the case when God delivered Lot from Sodom *for Abraham's sake* (19:29).

There is another interesting word about the prayer life of this generous man, Abraham. The first mention of the word *pray* in the Bible is in connection with his prayer for divine healing for Abimelech, his wife, and their maidservants (Gen 20:17-18). Abraham was mighty in prayer because he was generous in sharing with others. He had an "in" with God; therefore God healed all those for whom Abraham prayed. Since this is so, we must assume, in the light of Proverbs 21:13, that Abraham was not a stingy man.

There is another passage which bears heavily upon the subject of our present chapter. It has often been quoted, and, I fear, at times somewhat lightheartedly. Jesus said,

> Give, and it shall be given unto you; good measure, pressed down, and shaken together, and running over, shall men give into your bosom. For with the same measure that ye mete withal it shall be measured to you again (Lk 6:38).

The entire context in which this verse is given exhorts the followers of Christ to be considerate, gracious, forgiving, selfless, and generous toward others. They are to give and forgive, love and do good, be merciful and not condemn (vv. 27-38). And throughout that part of His discourse, Jesus stresses the idea of reciprocity.

Then, in accordance with this principle of love, Jesus exhorts His followers to exercise generosity and liberality. The whole idea is that we have no right to expect to receive if we are unwilling to give. "Give and it shall be given unto you." Conversely, if we will not give, it will not be given to us. The standard by which we deal with others shall be applied to us. Therefore it does not make sense when a miserly Christian asks anything of God. The boundless liberality of God never comes to those persons who give meagerly.

I am aware of the fact that many prosperous persons are

neither Christian nor religious. But that is another matter altogether. Neither the devil nor his followers are paupers. God makes "his sun to rise on the evil and on the good, and sendeth rain on the just and on the unjust" (Mt 5:45). When we speak of giving and receiving, we are not thinking merely of material things and money. We must be generous in sharing our time and strength and love with others, as well as our material wealth. The apostle Paul said,

> But this I say, He which soweth sparingly shall reap also sparingly; and he which soweth bountifully shall reap also bountifully. Every man according as he purposeth in his heart, so let him give; not grudgingly, or of necessity: for God loveth a cheerful giver (2 Co 9:6-7).

Here is a biblical principle which none of us can change. God wants to answer our prayers, but He Himself has determined the guidelines. Therefore it is senseless to pray for anything if we refuse to pray according to His rules. The mean and avaricious Christian should not expect that God will give him his requests. Now look at 2 Corinthians 9:8.

> And God is able to make all grace abound toward you; that ye, always having all sufficiency in all things, may abound to every good work.

God is able to make all grace abound toward *you*. But to whom does the *you* refer? To the "cheerful givers" (v.7). Are you a cheerful giver? Do you use what God gives to you in order that you "may abound to every good work"? Or do you use it to gratify your own desires and wants?

A few years ago I was in the process of writing a commentary on the first epistle of John. When I came to chapter 3 and verse 22, I paused to think. Look at that verse:

> And whatsoever we ask, we receive of him, because we keep his commandments, and do those things that are pleasing in his sight (1 Jn 3:22).

My first thoughts were, *Now that is a broad condition.*

What are those things that are pleasing in His sight? Then I saw that they were right there in the context. We are exhorted to "love the brethren" (3:14), and one way of proving our love is to share with them in their need (3:17-18). And when we obey this injunction, "Whatsoever we ask, we receive of him" (3:22) because such obedience is "pleasing in his sight."

This verse contains a great prayer promise, but it is conditioned upon our willingness to share with those who need help.

More than once I have listened to someone say, "Lord, supply our every need." Such a request can be a perfectly legitimate one, but on the other hand, it could be a foolish one. There are people who pray this prayer while failing in their stewardship responsibilities, or while spending their money extravagantly. Christians who rob God and who carelessly buy themselves into debt are praying senselessly every time they ask God to supply their needs. If we were to follow the sanctified wisdom of the Bible in the disbursing of all the money we receive, we could answer such a prayer ourselves. In the use of money, we can neither hoard selfishly nor squander carelessly if we expect God to grant us our requests.

The Bible contains another wonderful promise to liberal givers. Many Christians quote and claim it who have no right to do so. Here it is:

> But my God shall supply all your need according to his riches in glory by Christ Jesus (Phil 4:19).

Has it ever occured to you that here is a promise based upon a strict condition? It was not intended for all Christians, yet there are Christians trying to claim it who have no right to. That promise was given to a group of God's children who had sacrificed in order to share with Paul in his affliction and need (vv. 14-17). It was to those generous and liberal saints that the promise was given. They had helped Paul in his difficulty, sacrificing as no other church had sacrificed. Twice they sent a sacrificial gift to Paul when he was in Thessalonica, and because their self-denial had pleased God, they were now assured that God would supply all their needs.

Do we qualify to lay claim to Philippians 4:19? What sacrifice have we made to spread the gospel and support its ministers? God keeps accurate records, and He will supply the needs of His generous children.

The word *supply* means, literally, to fill full. Note that it is our needs that God promises to supply, not our wants. Sometimes the things we *want* are not really the things we *need*. God knows what we need better than we ourselves do. He knows *all* our needs, and He promises to fill them full. But let us not fail to meet the condition.

Any need that is created because of what we give, God will supply. Now, we should not give to get. We cannot bargain with God, as two persons might when making a reciprocal trade agreement. But a generous giving to the Lord does guarantee a generous getting from the Lord, one that will meet all our material and spiritual needs.

Human selfishness knows no bounds. Many of us do not want to be selfish, but sometimes we catch ourselves looking on things around us as though they were all there for our personal gratification and advantage. This is not so! It is doubly dangerous when we look upon God Himself as an easy touch and try to use Him to our greatest advantage. This is a misunderstanding of the meaning and purpose of prayer.

It does make sense to cultivate the grace of giving so that our prayers are not hindered.

12

Prayer and the Marriage Relationship

It does not make sense for a husband or wife to ask requests from God when the marriage relationship has broken down.

> Likewise, ye wives, be in subjection to your own husbands. . . . Likewise, ye husbands, dwell with them according to knowledge, giving honour unto the wife, as unto the weaker vessel, and as being heirs together of the grace of life; that your prayers be not hindered (1 Pe 3:1, 7).

The apostle Peter gets to the heart of this matter of prayer as it is affected by the husband-wife relationship. He warns all married couples that they had better shape up or suffer the hindrance of their own prayers.

He speaks first to wives. "Likewise, ye wives, be in subjection to your own husbands." Every wife needs to know that she must obey her husband and submit to him if prayer is to be meaningful. "Wives, submit yourselves unto your own husbands, as unto the Lord" (Eph 5:22). Ladies, this is God's command to you, and it is not optional; it is obligatory. If you cannot find it in your heart to submit to your husband for his sake, then you are to do it for the Lord's sake, *"in every thing"* (Eph 5:24). By refusing to submit to your husband, you are refusing to submit to the Lord, and such disobedience will hinder your prayer life.

How many Christian wives there are who rebel against this plain teaching of the Bible! To hear some wives teach a Sunday school class, or speak to a group of women, one might be led to believe that they are spiritual. But at home they refuse to take the subordinate place and to subject themselves to their own husbands, thereby showing that they are disobedient to God's Word and are carnal. And yet some of these women wonder why their prayer requests are not granted.

I read about a wife who developed a holiday tradition. Every Christmas she bought her husband a large, intricate jigsaw puzzle, and each year the entire family would combine their skill to meet the challenge of the puzzle. Of course, the wife would always hide the cover of the box, where the picture of the finished puzzle appeared, so that there would be no clue as to what the picture looked like.

But one year she left a cover exposed on the table. Her husband spread out the pieces of the puzzle and began the task of putting them together. For days he struggled without success. And then he discovered that the pieces of the puzzle on which he was working did not match the picture on the box. His wife had bought two puzzles and had switched the boxes. He had a false picture of what the finished puzzle would look like.

That story illustrates part of the problem in unhappy marriages. Young people are sometimes given a false picture of marriage. Instead of following the teaching of God's Word, they are led into devious paths. This is followed by a spiritual breakdown which seriously affects the prayer life.

The Christian wife should know that marriage is her chief career and the Bible her rule book. If she refuses to obey the rules, then she must suffer the spiritual losses which inevitably follow. Wives, are you submissive to your husband as the Bible teaches? Examine your heart honestly in the light of Scripture. If you are not getting your prayer requests, this could be the reason.

A Christian woman in Detroit expressed concern for her son's salvation. She claimed she never failed to pray at least once daily that God would save him. But his behavior became increasingly worse and eventually he ran afoul of the law. The mother became greatly distressed because God had not answered her prayer.

On one occasion I visited the home to offer assistance to those grieved parents. While there, I learned why her prayers were hindered. She was a domineering and rebellious wife.

A woman can pretend to be pious, be faithful in attending church services, take an active part in Christian work, and still refuse to treat her husband as the Bible instructs her. That woman hinders her own prayers. God will not respond to the heart that willfully disobeys His Word (Pr 28:9). When we do not get the requests for which we ask, the fault lies with us, not with God. Prayer is a mighty force, but God's laws govern prayer. "Wives, submit yourselves unto your own husbands, as it is fit in the Lord" (Col 3:18).

A wife who is not in the right relationship to her husband cannot be in the right relationship to God. The wife who wants to dominate her husband, and who pouts and stirs up a fuss when she cannot have her way, is spiritually immature. No carnal Christian has power with God in prayer.

A nagging wife will create an unhappy atmosphere in the home. "It is better to dwell in the wilderness, than with a contentious and an angry woman" (Pr 21:19). Every husband has needs, but a rebellious and stubborn wife is unable to help meet his needs.

God has ordained that the husband be the spiritual head in the home. Peter wrote, "Likewise, ye husbands, dwell with them according to knowledge, giving honour unto the wife, as unto the weaker vessel, and as being heirs together of the grace of life: that your prayers be not hindered" (1 Pe 3:7).

This exhortation to husbands begins by telling them that they should live with their wives "according to knowledge."

Now, that is not an easy assignment for some men. Getting to know and understand some women might call for a lifetime of study, and even then the effort could be most frustrating.

But what does God mean when He tells husbands to live with their wives "according to knowledge"? The first thing the husband should know is that the wife is the "weaker vessel." That does not mean that she is inferior mentally or spiritually, but that she is weaker physically. This is the way God made her; therefore the weaker must depend on the stronger. No husband will ever fully understand his wife, though he may think he does. But one thing he must know: his wife is the weaker of the two, and therefore she depends on her husband for protection and provision. The knowledge Peter speaks about is not an acquisition of information, not knowledge in the abstract, but rather intelligent considera-tion. It is this knowledge which is so important in establish-ing a right relationship. The husband who fails to acknowl-edge the seriousness of his obligation hinders his own prayers.

The exhortation to the husband continues with the words, "giving honour unto the wife." Here, the "honour" is the esteem or advantage the husband gives to his wife instead of claiming it for himself. The Christian husband and wife are "heirs together of the grace of life," and grace will be in evidence in the husband's life when he displays proper re-spect and regard for his wife.

"The husband is the head of the wife, even as Christ is the head of the church" (Eph 5:23). However, male headship does not mean that the man is always right and his wife is always wrong. It does mean, "Husbands, love your wives, even as Christ also loved the church, and gave himself for it" (Eph 5:25). Men, do not overlook those words, *as Christ also loved the church, and gave himself for it*. Christ's love was self-sacrificing: He died for us while we were still sinners (Ro 5:8). It was that love to which you and I responded as sinners. Why do we believers love Christ? "We love him, because he first loved us'' (1 Jn 4:19). We received love, and we responded to love.

This is the way God made woman. When she receives love from her husband, she will respond to his love. A husband receives from his wife what he gives to her. And when he fails to love his wife as Christ loved him, he cuts off the power of prayer and threatens his marriage.

Warren phoned me one morning for an appointment. He said the matter was urgent and that he would like to talk with me on his lunch hour that day. He was thirty-four years old and married to a fine Christian girl.

At ten minutes past twelve, quite nervous and upset, he came to my office. I invited him to sit down, with the suggestion that we first ask God for guidance. I prayed briefly, after which he told me about his problem.

"Pastor, I have decided to leave Chris because of the way she has been bugging me lately. I find it hard to love her."

Actually, Warren had put the cart before the horse. After three counselling sessions, the real problem came to the surface. Chris was partly at fault, but the real problem lay with Warren himself. The pressure at work, brought on by the increasing demands upon him, had stirred up tension and irritability within him. He had not been fully aware of the change in himself, and so he had failed to take the initiative in being loving and considerate. Chris had responded in kind. She had become cool and easily found fault.

The result was a serious hindrance in their prayer life. On Warren's second visit, we reviewed together 1 Corinthians 13, the well-known love chapter. After reading the description of love presented by Paul, we discussed how love behaves.

1. *Love suffereth long* (v.4). Love is slow to become angry, slow to become offended, slow to become indignant.
2. *Love is kind* (v.4). Love is positive. Love shows

gentleness, tenderness, goodness of heart, and is pleasant.

3. *Love envieth not* (v.4). Love does not begrudge; therefore it will not be jealous or selfish of another.

4. *Love vaunteth not itself* (v.4). Love is not rash or boastful; therefore it is not guilty of vainglory.

5. *Love is not puffed up* (v.4). Love does not become inflated with pride or self-importance.

6. *Love does not behave itself unseemly* (v.5). Love is never discourteous or impolite, and is not lacking in good manners.

7. *Love seeketh not her own* (v.5). Love insists on no rights of its own but will forfeit all for the one it loves.

8. *Love is not easily provoked* (v.5). Love will not be excited or stirred up to anger, will not be aroused to resentment.

9. *Love thinketh no evil* (v.5). Love looks for the best and not the worst; it magnifies the good points and minimizes the weaknesses.

10. *Love rejoiceth not in iniquity, but rejoiceth in the truth* (v.6). Love is never glad to see the wrong in others, only the right.

11. *Love beareth all things* (v.7). Love silently and sweetly puts up with all it cannot approve. Love will bear and forbear.

12. *Love believeth all things* (v.7). Love will trust and not doubt, accept and not be suspicious.

13. *Love hopeth all things* (v.7). Love will not quit, will not give up to a divorce.

14. *Love endureth all things* (v.7). Love rides out the storms of life, withstands every disappointment.

15. *Love never faileth* (v.8). Love will never leave off, never lose its grip. Love must succeed.

After Warren and I had gone over these fifteen descriptions of love, he said, "Pastor, I have never loved Chris like that, but with God's help I will start at once.'' He phoned her from my office, told her he loved her, and apologized for his wrong attitude.

One of the first things Warren and Chris had done when they were married was to make a prayer list. Included in that list was the request for the salvation of Warren's father, who continued in unbelief. Less than three months after reestablishing their marriage on the above principles, Warren's father was saved.

It does make sense for Christian husbands and wives to live by God's rules so that their "prayers be not hindered."

13

Prayer and Fasting

*It does not make sense to ignore the spiritual exercise of
fasting as an aid to prayer.*

Prayer and fasting are linked together in several New
Testament passages (see Mt 17:21; Mk 9:29; Lk 2:37; Ac
10:30-32; 13:2-3; 14:23; 1 Co 7:5). The verb *to fast* (Gr.,
nesteuo) means to abstain from eating.

Fasting is a religious practice enjoined upon Jews (Ac
27:9), and practiced by Roman Catholics and others during
Lent, a forty-day period (Sundays excluded) from Ash Wednesday till Easter.

Before we look at fasting in its relation to prayer, we
should examine the following words of our Lord:

> Moreover when ye fast, be not, as the hypocrites, of a sad
> countenance: for they disfigure their faces, that they may
> appear unto men to fast. Verily I say unto you, They have
> their reward. But thou, when thou fastest, anoint thine head,
> and wash thy face; that thou appear not unto men to fast, but
> unto thy Father which is in secret; and thy Father, which
> seeth in secret, shall reward thee openly (Mt 6:16-18).

The religious observance of fasting was practiced often by
the Pharisees (Mt 9:14), at least twice weekly (Lk 18:12).
Christ assumed that His disciples fasted; therefore He did

not say *if* but *when*, as though He expected that there would
be times when they would fast.

Now look closely at the context in which our Lord's words
about fasting appear. He had just completed His now famous
words about prayer (Mt 6:5-15), after which He launched
into the discourse on fasting. So it seems that there is a
relation between the two.

In prayer we draw near to God; in fasting we detach
ourselves from something that could keep us from praying.
There will come times in the experience of the truly spiritual
child of God, when he will be so taken up with the burden to
pray, that he will not have time for nor give thought to eating.
The need to pray will become such a burden that he will
forget all else but prayer. If at such a time he yields to the
appetite of the flesh and gives up praying, he loses power.
Our Lord's disciples learned their lesson the hard way, for in
their ineffectiveness in casting out a demon, He said to them,
"This kind can come forth by nothing, but by prayer and
fasting" (Mk 9:29).

When we fast, we must guard against a corrupt motive.
Jesus warned against hypocrisy in fasting. Fasting so as to
impress men is not accepted by God. If we hang out the sign
in order that others will take notice that we have lost weight,
thereby impressing our selected audience with the sacrifice
we have made, then that is all the reward we get (Mt 6:16).
God detests hypocrisy. If we merely focus men's attention
upon ourselves, the act has no merit with God.

Why might anyone want to "appear unto men to fast"?
Possibly to impress them with his discipline and self-control.
Or else to let others know that he is mourning for sin of which
he has repented. In the Old Testament, fasting suggested the
repentant humbling of the soul before God. But it is possible
for one to fast and to have the praises of men in so doing, and
thereby disregard God. All such is false piety. Do your
fasting in secret, and live normally before your fellowmen.

The motive must be right if we are going to fast. Apart from health reasons, fasting is a spiritual exercise between God and the individual. Fasting, in the true sense, does not mean looking upon the material necessities of life as unclean. It does mean that at times we need to concentrate more on worshiping God in prayer, and so for a time we lay aside even those things which are both allowable and needful.

How often and to what extent do we think about fasting today? This whole subject seems to have dropped out of our thinking. Possibly this is due to the fact that the New Testament epistles have very little to say about it. Certainly, it is never enjoined upon the church of Christ. When our Lord taught fasting, He did not command it directly, but He taught it indirectly. He approved it but did not prohibit it. He Himself fasted forty days and forty nights when He went into the wilderness to be tempted of Satan (Mt 4:1-2).

The apostles found fasting to be profitable. When the church at Antioch sent out Paul and Barnabas on their first preaching mission, it did so only after a period of prayer and fasting. Luke wrote:

> As they ministered to the Lord, and fasted, the Holy Ghost said, Separate me Barnabas and Saul for the work whereunto I have called them. And when they had fasted and prayed, and laid their hands on them, they sent them away (Ac 13:2-3).

Fasting was an accepted practice in the early church.

What exactly is the reason for fasting? In order to find an answer to this question, we must consider man in his three constituent parts: spirit, mind, and body. Since God created man a tripartite being, it follows that all of the parts are intimately related to each other. Moreover, there is a reciprocal action between all parts, whereby each part is affected by the others. We all know that the condition of our bodies has a direct bearing upon the function of the mind and of the spirit. Have you ever attempted to concentrate on praying earnestly and specifically about something when your body was in severe pain? A bad toothache, for example, can affect the whole personality.

Prayer is basically a spiritual exercise. Our Lord said, "God is a Spirit: and they that worship him must worship him in spirit and in truth" (Jn 4:24). If there is an urgent need to pray about a specific matter, there could be an urgent need to abstain from food, drink, and all else for spiritual purposes. The need to pray is so demanding that I go about the matter of drawing near to God without giving thought to food or drink. It seems to me that this is the right way to fast.

Fasting should not be done in a mechanical or legalistic manner. This does not refer to moderation in eating as a disciplinary function; that is scriptural and good (1 Co 9:24-27), and something too many Christians neglect. That kind of fasting can be mechanical and routine. But fasting for spiritual purposes cannot be legalized nor systemized. Millions of people have abstained from eating meat on Friday and during Lent because they were taught to do so. They have done it as a matter of rule. This is religious, but certainly not in keeping with the scriptural teaching on fasting. These people expect certain benefits or results, but that understanding of fasting has no biblical basis.

I know a Christian woman who reminds me from time to time that she fasts one day every week. Now, I will not argue against some physical benefits that might accrue from such fasting, but such programming of one's life does not in itself result in spiritual blessing.

I will go a step further and apply my comments to prayer. For many years I have been close to another person who often reminds me not to call between eight and nine o'clock in the morning, because that time is set aside for prayer. I certainly cannot find any fault with the idea of praying between eight and nine every morning, but if I were to plan this in my schedule for each day, and then pray merely to follow my schedule, I would not necessarily be praying effectively. Neither prayer nor fasting are an end in themselves. The wrong way to pray and fast is to do it mechanically and then call attention to the fact that I am doing it.

There are some people in the modern charismatic movement who make much of fasting, and they are not slow in letting you know about it. One testimony was published as follows:

> I have been a Christian for fourteen years, but my Christian life was dull and meaningless. I attended church regularly but I can't say that it did much for me. Then I met a Christian where I work who told me she fasted one day every week, and on that day she always spoke in tongues. I tried it, and I can only say if you really want the blessing, start fasting.

Now, that is unscriptural. It is an example of experience that is not based on the truth of God's Word. It is not scriptural to practice fasting as a means of obtaining an experience, even though that experience appears to be a blessing. The Christian must start with truth, and then make certain that his experience is in conformity with the truth. Not all the experiences that Christians have are true Christian experiences. Experiences can appeal to the flesh and give a certain satisfaction that is soulish and not spiritual. We must be very careful not to confuse the soulish with the spiritual. I do not wish to set myself up as a judge, but I do feel that some people who practice fasting have crossed the border line from the spiritual to the soulish, or fleshly. Fasting with regularity does not guarantee true righteousness and spirituality.

Is fasting for Christians today? I find no specific instruction given in the Bible. However, there may be times when the burden to pray becomes so great that we will give ourselves to prayer and not think once of the needful food and drink. If you are constrained to pray and fast, do not divulge it to anyone. Keep it within an intimate and personal relationship with our heavenly Father. This is what our Lord had in mind when He said, "But thou, when thou fastest . . .

appear not unto men to fast, but unto thy Father which is in secret: and thy Father, which seeth in secret, shall reward thee openly'' (Mt 6:17-18).

Fasting has a certain spiritual value when practiced in keeping with the teaching of Christ. If we are faced with insurmountable problems or overpowering tasks, then let us give ourselves to the holy business of prayer. If anything ordinarily natural and legitimate, such as food, or drink, must be laid aside, God has the record, and He will reward us in due time.

It does make sense to fast and pray in keeping with the teaching of Christ.

14

History's Most Debated Prayer

WE NOW COME to a consideration of what is commonly called the Lord's Prayer. This much loved, yet much discussed and debated prayer was possibly given on two separate occasions and under different circumstances. We see it first in the Sermon on the Mount (Mt 6:9-13), and second at an unnamed, "certain place," when one of Christ's disciples requested, "Lord, teach us to pray" (Lk 11:1-4).

Anyone who writes on this so-called Lord's Prayer has stepped on a battleground. In the first place, the title "The Lord's Prayer" is inaccurate, because it is without any biblical foundation. Our Lord never prayed this prayer, nor could He ever have prayed it, because of the petition, "Forgive us our debts [sins]" (Mt 6:12; cf. Lk 11:4). The Lord Jesus was sinless; therefore He never needed to confess sin nor ask for forgiveness. He never took an offering to the temple as a sacrifice for sin. He was the only sinless man ever to appear on earth. "In him is no sin" (1 Jn 3:5); He "knew no sin" (2 Co 5:21); He is "holy, harmless, undefiled, separate from sinners" (Heb 7:26). Only He could say, "Which of you convinceth me of sin?" (Jn 8:46). Christ was without sin in every respect (Jn 14:30; Heb 4:15; 1 Pe 2:22). To state it accurately, the *real* Lord's Prayer is the prayer Jesus prayed in John 17.

However, the more serious controversy revolves around

two extreme views of the Sermon on the Mount, in which the prayer appears. There are those who look upon the Sermon on the Mount as the distilled essence of Christianity, containing all we need to know for right living. The liberal theologian holds to this view. He regards the Sermon on the Mount as a means of salvation for all, individuals and nations, the churched and the unchurched. This view is popular with liberals because blood theology, which to them is repulsive, does not appear in the sermon.

This view of the sermon is not acceptable. It makes salvation to be of works, apart from God's grace. There is no mention of regeneration, redemption, atonement, or justification — those basic and essential themes relating to salvation. But the discourse was not given as a guide to salvation, either for the individual or for society. To make the Sermon on the Mount a way of salvation would be to preach a gospel of human works. One liberal has said, "All I need is the Sermon on the Mount. You can destroy the rest of the Bible, as far as I am concerned."

The other extreme view is the ultradispensational concept that the Sermon has no meaning for Christians today. There are good and godly teachers of God's Word who insist that the Sermon has in it no validity for believers in this present dispensation of grace. These brethren insist that the teaching of the sermon is for the kingdom age only, and must therefore be set aside to await its fulfillment when Christ comes to earth to reign. One teacher insists, "The Sermon relates only to the future Messianic Kingdom in the future Millennium."

However, several objections can be offered. There are some things in the sermon that do not make sense if it is for the kingdom age only. For example, if the kingdom and the King have come, why pray, "Thy kingdom come" (Mt 6:10)? Furthermore, the presence of persecution (5:10), the adversary (5:25), anxiety over material needs (6:25-34) and false teachers (7:15) are all contrary to other biblical descrip-

tions of the nature of the kingdom. The millennium is characterized as a time in which God's truth will prevail (Is 11:9; Jer
31:33-34), righteousness shall flourish (Ps 72:7; Is 11:3-5),
and peace will reign (Ps 72:7; Is 2:4; Mic 4:3).

In its primary interpretation, the sermon is not addressed
to the church. Not once did Jesus mention the Holy Spirit or
the church per se. Moreover, the words *kingdom* and *church*
are not to be used synonymously. Those who consider the
kingdom to be the church must ignore the dispensational
interpretation of Scripture and fall back upon the spiritualizing method of interpretation.

It seems best to apply here the principle found in 2
Timothy 3:16:

> All scripture is given by inspiration of God, and is profitable
> for doctrine, for reproof, for correction, for instruction in
> righteousness.

We must never miss the importance of any passage of Scripture in its application to us today. The Sermon on the Mount
is not a standard of conduct to be applied to unregenerated
men, nor is it the modus operandi for Christian conduct
today. Nevertheless, it does contain a standard of ethics and
practices which are not contrary to the principles of Christian conduct. We Christians should consider the principles
which Christ gave in the sermon. If He is reigning in our
lives, the truth of the sermon will find an application in our
behavior. In our age of relaxed, careless living, we Christians need to apply the lessons to life so as to overcome the
prevailing shallowness which characterizes so many of us.

The call to prayer is not an easy assignment. I have not
found it easy, and most of my Christian friends tell me the
same. So then, let us do now as the disciples did when, after
hearing Christ pray, they said to Him, "Lord, teach us to
pray" (Lk 11:1).

When He taught them about prayer, our Lord sounded a
warning against three perils:

1. THE PERIL OF PROMINENT PRAYING

> And when thou prayest, thou shalt not be as the hypocrites are: for they love to pray standing in the synagogues and in the corners of the streets, that they may be seen of men. Verily, I say unto you, They have their reward (Mt 6:5).

Here Jesus is exposing the hypocrisy in praying that is done in public, where an audience is assured. He is not condemning praying in public, for there is a place for public prayer. What He is condemning is the prayer offered in public that should be offered in secret. He is exposing the sin of telling ourselves we are worshiping God when in reality we are worshiping ourselves. This is the worst form of hypocrisy.

Prominent praying is a false way of praying. The hypocrite wanted to be known among his fellowmen as a man of prayer, so on his way to the temple he paused in the public square and dropped to his knees, thereby impressing others with the idea that he could not wait to get to the temple to pray. He accomplished what he set out to do, and that, said Jesus, was his reward — his only reward. He prayed to be seen of men, and men saw and heard him pray. What he desired, he obtained.

2. THE PERIL OF PRETENSE IN PRAYING

> Woe unto you, scribes and Pharisees, hypocrites! for ye devour widows' houses, and for a pretence make long prayer: therefore ye shall receive the greater damnation (Mt 23:14).

The word *pretence* is the translation of *prophasis*, meaning cloak. It suggests the show of something so as to disguise one's real self or motives. This is the terrible act of going through the motions of praying in an attempt to cover up some sin. The prayer is merely a pretense, or cloak, to conceal the real man. The danger of this kind of praying is so subtle that we must ever be on guard lest it creep up on us.

Some of the scribes and Pharisees were guilty of offering

prayers for a pretense, so our Lord pronounced a woe upon them. They appeared to be pious in their prayers, but they fell short of God's standard of righteousness in their everyday behavior.

I remember some people talking about a certain business man who attended Bible conferences and prayer meetings with regularity and who was always ready to offer prayer. That man had the reputation of being hard on his tenants and of driving a hard bargain in a business transaction. He went out of his way to impress people with his ability to pray eloquently, but his prayers were nothing more than a cloak, a pretense. Nobody was favorably impressed.

3. THE PERIL OF PROLONGED PRAYERS

In this same passage, Jesus spoke about those persons who make "long prayer." There are people who attach great importance to long prayers, thereby leading others to believe that the more saintly Christians spend much of their time on their knees, praying. Therefore we may tend to think that the way to become a great Christian is to keep our eyes on the clock so that we can report how much time we have spent in prayer. Frankly, I would question whether public prayers should be long. The prayer in Matthew 6:9-13 contains only sixty-six words, and there is a vast range of truth compressed into those few words.

At mealtime during a certain Bible conference I attended, the conference director called on a man to offer thanks for the food. That prayer led us on a journey from Egypt to Canaan, and when we finally reached Canaan, the hot food on the table had become cold. (Incidentally, in the process he had forgotten to thank God for the food.)

I wondered if perhaps the brother did only a little praying in private and had taken advantage of the situation to catch up on his prayers. I did not appreciate his taking my time and spoiling my meal to do in public what he could have done privately. I am not judging, but I do commend my thoughts to you for your consideration.

We come now to a consideration of our Lord's teaching concerning prayer, one of the most essential aspects of our Christian life. When a man is speaking to God, he is engaged in the highest activity of the human soul. Most things we do in the Christian life are easier than prayer. It is not difficult to give time or money if I have time and money to give. It is not difficult to preach a sermon if I have prepared that sermon and I have something to say. But prayer, which is speaking to God, is the ultimate test.

I question whether our Lord's objective was to provide a prayer to be recited by His followers. He did not say, "Recite these words verbatim," but, "After this manner therefore pray ye" (Mt 6:9). It seems clear that He was giving a formulary, or model, of how to pray and for what to pray. We do not have here sixty-six words merely to be memorized and recited. I am not saying that we should not memorize and recite these five verses of Scripture any more than I would tell you not to memorize and recite the Twenty-third Psalm. I am simply stating that this was not our Lord's main objective. What we have here is a pattern for our prayers, and the pattern contains certain principles. What we should do is accept the principles, apply them to our own lives, and work them out in our own experience. The words we use in our prayers may vary widely, but the principles never change. If my prayers are to be acceptable to God, then I must follow the principles.

The prayer contains six petitions. The first three have to do with God and His glory; the last three relate to man and his needs. This is the divine order for proper praying, and it cannot be reversed. In true prayer, God and His glory claim top priority. Selfishness and self-centeredness are out. Everything the Christian does should be for the glory of God (1 Co 10:31), and prayer is the Christian's highest exercise.

GOD'S PRIORITY: *Thy* name be hallowed.
                Thy kingdom come.
                Thy will be done.

MAN'S POVERTY: *Us* give daily bread.
               Us forgive.
               Us lead not into temptation.
               Us deliver from evil.

Before considering the petitions in detail, the following outline is given so as to present a bird's-eye view of the whole:

I. Petitions relating to the nature of God
   A. Our relationship to God: "Our Father which art in heaven"
   B. Our reverence for God: "Hallowed be thy name"
   C. Our resignation before God: "Thy kingdom come. Thy will be done"

II. Petitions relating to the needs of man
   A. A request for provision: "Give us this day our daily bread"
   B. A request for pardon: "Forgive us our debts, as we forgive our debtors"
   C. A request for protection: "Lead us not into temptation, but deliver us from evil"

I. PETITIONS RELATING TO THE NATURE OF GOD

A. OUR RELATIONSHIP TO GOD

Our Father which art in heaven

Actually, that is the invocation. It tells us that all prayer to God is predicated on a right relationship to Him. Prayer is for God's family, of which He is the Father, and none save His children can call Him Father.

Is God your Father? Some of you might consider my

question to be superfluous and tell me that God is the Father of all mankind. Well, if that is your understanding of God and His relationship to the human race, you are only partially correct. At the court of the Areopagites on Mar's Hill, Paul did agree that we are all His offspring (Ac 17:28), but there Paul is speaking only of God's relation to man as his Creator. Malachi also stresses this relationship (Mal 2:10). But man is not now what he was when God created him. Jesus said to some of the religious leaders in His own day, "Ye are of your father the devil" (Jn 8:44).

The word *father* denotes paternity. The father is the one responsible for the birth of a child—in this case, the new birth. Without this spiritual birth from above, no man can enter the family of God (Jn 3:5). Jesus said, "Ye must be born again" (Jn 3:7). The necessity for the second birth grows out of the fact that all of Adam's offspring are born in sin (Ps 51:5; Ro 5:12). The second birth occurs when the believing sinner trusts Christ for salvation. Paul wrote to those who received Christ, saying, "For ye are all the children of God by faith in Christ Jesus" (Gal 3:26). The Bible does not support the liberal idea of the universal fatherhood, of God.

The real meaning of this word "Father" as used here is caught in our Lord's prayer in Gethsemane when He prayed, "Abba, Father" (Mk 14:36). Paul used the word *Abba* twice when he encouraged us to pray. This word *Abba* was the word by which a small child would address his father. William Barclay says,

> There is only one possible English translation of this word in any ordinary use of it, and that is "Daddy". Of course, to translate it that way in the New Testament would sound bizarre and grotesque, but it does at once give us the atmosphere in which we come to God; we come to God with the simple trust and confidence with which a little child comes to a father whom he knows and loves and trusts.

B. Our Reverence for God

Hallowed be thy name

The word *hallow* (Gr. *hagiazo*) means to revere or to sanctify. In the New Testament, *hallowed* is used with reference to the name of God only, appearing in Matthew 6:9 and Luke 11:2. Modern translations and paraphrases sometimes detract from the real meaning of this word by offering substitutes for it, when actually there is no word more suited than *hallowed*. The words *holy, sanctified, venerated,* and *honored* are all good terms. I prefer *hallowed*. Nothing that we can do or say can add to the holiness of God's name, because His name represents Himself, and He is supremely the Holy One. It is an act of irreverence to doubt God, distrust Him, or degrade His name.

In our times, there has arisen a lighthearted, flippant approach to God. Too frequently, even in Christian circles, God's name is not treated as holy or held in reverence. I fear that too many professing Christians have never learned that God's name stands for His nature, His character, who and what He is. I detect a growing irreverence in both direct and indirect references to God. I do not like it. Millions of Roman Catholics and Protestants recite regularly, "Hallowed be thy name," and are not aware of the fact that the name here is a reference to God Himself, in all His attributes, attitudes, and actions.

It has pleased the Creator of heaven and earth and man and angels to reveal Himself in several ways. God has made Himself known in creation (Ps 19:1), in the Scriptures, and in Jesus Christ. But He has also given remarkable disclosures of Himself in His many names and titles. Therefore we are under obligation to give the reverence which His unique character deserves and demands. Wherever disrespect is shown toward God's name, there cannot be true reverence.

God's name should never be profaned. To profane is to unhallow, to permit to be desecrated or degraded. Any person who pollutes God's name has crossed the threshold from the holy to the unholy. Usually such profanity issues forth in the words spoken by the man on the street. However, I agree with the late Dr. G. Campbell Morgan who said, ''I am more afraid of the blasphemy of the sanctuary than the blasphemy of the street.'' It is more tragic when men and women go to God's house of worship and recite and sing His hallowed name with the lips while the heart is not clean.

God's name should always be praised. It is praised outwardly in public worship, in prayers, singing, and recitation of creeds. But if the outward form does not represent the true spirit of our hearts, we have failed to hallow His name. We must hallow the name of God in our everyday behavior. If our behavior does not bring honor to God, so as to attract others to Him, we have failed. God's name should be hallowed in us; it should be regarded as holy in our thoughts, words, and deeds. It is vain to recite the petition if our life is not a witness to our faith in Him and our love for Him. Let this petition be a challenge to total commitment to the Father, to Jesus Christ the Son, and to the Holy Spirit.

C. OUR RESIGNATION BEFORE GOD

Thy Kingdom come. Thy will be done

There are two rival kingdoms in the world, the kingdom of God and the kingdom of Satan. Those persons in Satan's kingdom are ruled by Satan; God's children are subject to God's rule. When a child of the devil becomes a child of God, there is a switch from one kingdom to another. Paul thanked God, ''Who hath delivered us from the power of darkness, and hath translated us into the kingdom of his dear Son'' (Col 1:13). In one sense, particularly in the New Testament, the kingdom is set forth as being a present reality. Jesus said, ''The kingdom of God is within you'' (Lk 17:21). Actually, the kingdom of God is any sphere over which God rules. If we are resigned before God to give Him full allegiance and to do only His will, we can say that His kingdom has come to us.

This is what our Lord had in mind when He said, "Seek ye first the kingdom of God, and his righteousness" (Mt 6:33). The Christian does this when he subjects himself to God's rule. The moment we pray, "Thy kingdom come. Thy will be done," we are at once submitting ourselves to implicit obedience to the will of God. The kingdom of God is present in every believer in whose heart Christ reigns.

But in another sense, the kingdom is still future. It is future for those who are still in Satan's kingdom of darkness but who will be saved. We must pray for those poor souls who are in bondage to sin and Satan, that they will be delivered and will submit to the authority and lordship of Jesus Christ. So this petition includes men and women and boys and girls who are lost.

But in still another sense, God's kingdom must be established throughout the whole earth. That day is approaching when the King will come to earth and establish His throne. That will be the climactic coming of the kingdom. We should have a genuine desire that the kingdom of God and of Christ will come to the hearts of men now, but the petition goes beyond that. It is a prayer for the literal coming of Christ. And the logical consequence of His coming will be the doing of His will on earth as it is done now in heaven. It is in the plan of God that His will shall one day prevail here among His creatures. "Even so, come, Lord Jesus" (Rev 22:20).

II. Petitions Relating to the Needs of Man

A. A Request for Provision

Give us this day our daily bread

The average Christian in our affluent society feels it unnecessary to take this request seriously while the freezer is stocked with food and the supermarket is close by. Why pray to God for food when I have a year's supply on hand? But whether one has little or much of this world's goods, the petition is designed to teach us that God is our source of supply.

The request is for our *daily* bread. There is no thought of storing up for years ahead but rather of reliance upon God for our immediate needs. It is a petition for daily bread, for those things necessary to hold body and soul together for *this* day. There could be a lot more in this petition, but I do at least see here the importance of living one day at a time and trusting God to provide the needs for that one day. By asking for our daily bread, we are simply acknowledging that our times are in God's hands. We do not know what a day will bring forth, but we know the one who does know, and we can go on trusting Him one day at a time.

Bread is the necessary staff of life, and God knows how much we need and when we need it. We do not pray for our needs because God is not aware of them. He knows what they are before we ask. But we do need that contact with our heavenly Father, who is the Creator and Sustainer of life. The value and the importance of prayer is that it keeps us in fellowship with God, a relationship that He desires and that we need. If God gave us all the necessities of our entire lifetime in one large gift at one time, He might not hear from some of us again. Through prayer we learn our dependence upon God.

Then, too, the request is for *our* (not *my*) daily bread. There is no place in true praying for the typical selfishness that pervades so much of life. I am not alone in my need. The staple necessities for the coming day are not limited to "me and my wife, our son and his wife, us four and no more." I have no right to ask anything for myself that I will not ask for others. Prayer teaches us our debt to our fellowman.

There is still another thought that comes to my mind. The petition, "Give us this day our daily bread," does not mean that God will do for me what He expects me to do for myself. He has already decreed, "In the sweat of thy face shalt thou eat bread'' (Gen 3:19), meaning that man must toil for the necessities of life. If I sit down, fold my hands, do nothing, and merely wait for God to spoon-feed me, I will starve. But after I have done my day's work and have earned my wages, I am still aware of the fact that my heavenly Father gave me life and sustained me so that I could go about my daily tasks. Back of my life and that bread on my table is my Father in heaven, so I will thank Him daily and continue to depend on Him.

B. A REQUEST FOR PARDON

*And forgive us our debts, as we
forgive our debtors*

As we recall the goodness and mercy of God in providing us with the daily necessities of life, it is only right that we admit that we do not deserve it. After all, we are indebted to God; He is not indebted to us. We wronged Him by sinning against Him. The debts in this petition are not monetary debts, but debts of a moral and spiritual nature. Luke uses the terms *debts* and *sins* interchangeably — "And forgive us our sins; for we also forgive every one that is indebted to us" (Lk 11:4).

It is true that we believers in Christ have experienced once-for-all forgiveness and are thereby established positionally in Him. "In whom we have . . . the forgiveness of sins, according to the riches of his grace" (Eph 1:7; see also 1 Jn 2:12). Yet we do sin, and therefore we need daily cleansing and forgiveness so that our fellowship with our heavenly Father may continue.

When we sin, whether the sin be one of commission or of omission, we incur an obligation upon ourselves. Every time we sin, we break fellowship with God, and this robs both God and the one who sins. The forgiveness in regeneration is a once-for-all experience, but the forgiveness of daily sanctification, or cleansing, must be experienced as often as we sin. Sin always breaks fellowship; it needs cleansing and forgiveness from God, who is both giving and forgiving.

The petition says, "Forgive us . . . *as* we forgive." This does not mean that we earn forgiveness by forgiving others; it is not a merit system. The point is simply that we have no right to expect God to forgive us our sins if we are unwilling to forgive those persons who have wronged us. Immediately following the *Amen* of the prayer, we have Christ's statement, "For if ye forgive men their trespasses, your heavenly Father will also forgive you: But if ye forgive not men their trespasses, neither will your Father forgive your trespasses" (Mt 6:14-15). The basic fact is that the Christian who is unforgiving has created a barrier between God and himself. This is why the unforgiving debtor in our Lord's parable could not expect forgiveness for himself (Mt 18:23-35). One condition of forgiveness is a forgiving spirit. The person who will not forgive had better hope that he will never sin. "When ye stand praying, forgive" (Mk 11:25).

C. A REQUEST FOR PROTECTION

> *Lead us not into temptation, but*
> *deliver us from evil*

In the preceding petition, the request was that sins already committed might be remitted, but here we have a plea to be delivered from falling into new sins.

There are variations in the translation of the words, *Lead us not into temptation*. Whatever difficulty one encounters here, we know for certain that God never tempts man to do evil. The Scripture is clear on this point. "Let no man say when he is tempted, I am tempted of God: for God cannot be tempted with evil, neither tempteth he any man" (Ja 1:13). It is true that man's life on earth is one continuous temptation. But on the other hand, I cannot conceive of God seducing man to sin.

The noun *temptation* (Gr. *peirasomos*) is by no means easy to translate. Usually it means to test or to prove. The verb form is *peirazein,* used by Paul when he said, "Examine [*peirazein*] yourselves, whether ye be in the faith" (2 Co 13:5). It was used in connection with the scribes and Pharisees who maliciously cross-examined Jesus so as to entrap Him (Mt 16:1; 19:3; 22:18).

However, the same word is used of Satan, who is called the tempter (Gr. *ho peirazon*) in Matthew 4:3 and 1 Thessalonians 3:5). Paul warned Christian husbands and wives not to deny each other conjugal rights, except by mutual agreement, "that Satan tempt you not for your incontinency" (1 Co 7:5). Whenever the word *tempt* is used to mean luring a person to commit sin, it refers to temptation originating with the devil. God will never deliberately do anything to draw a child of His into sin. Personally, I prefer to render the petition, "Do not permit us to be led into temptation."

There are those persons who hold to the idea that all evil is woven into the pattern of our lives by God, thereby ascribing to God full responsibility for man's sin. But this is the very thing that God condemns (Ja 1:13). God subjects His children to testing, but Satan seduces them into sin.

The petition in the prayer is primarily one for protection. It accepts the danger of temptation, acknowledges our deficiency in dealing with it, and asks for deliverance from it. To sum it all up, this petition reflects dependence upon God for protection both from evil and from the evil one. And after all, our heavenly Father is the mighty deliverer. He is able to deliver us both here and now, and finally and fully when He takes us to heaven.

Do you want to be kept from evil? Then do what our Lord told His disciples to do: "Watch and pray, that ye enter not into temptation" (Mt 26:41).

At the end of the prayer we read what I am going to call the doxology:

> *For thine is the kingdom, and the*
> *power, and the glory, forever, Amen.*

Later manuscripts, discovered after the King James Version was translated, omit these words. They are not included in the Revised Version. But this need not alarm us. The words fit into the spirit of the prayer and teachings elsewhere in the Bible. Read David's prayer in 1 Chronicles 29:11, and you will see what I mean:

> Thine, O LORD, is the greatness, and the power, and the glory, and the victory, and the majesty: for all that is in the heaven and in the earth is thine; thine is the kingdom, O LORD, and thou art exalted as head above all.

The kingdom is Christ's, and when it comes in its fullness and finality, the King Himself will have come. It will not come as the result of ecumenical effort nor by means of man's maneuvering. The kingdom will come with the personal return of Christ to earth. Then all creation will know His power and His glory.

15

The Prayer Life of Jesus

OUR LORD JESUS CHRIST instructed His disciples to pray, and in so doing He taught them by precept. But the greater impact was made upon their lives when they watched and heard Him pray. His prayer life was an illustration of how they should pray, teaching them by His example. We preach, and then we struggle to practice that which we have preached, but Jesus preached what He practiced. He taught much about prayer, but He also loved to pray. Praying was a natural part of His life; to Him it was like breathing.

Let us spend a few minutes in the school of prayer and learn how Jesus prayed. It is important that we study what He said about prayer, but it is equally important that we know how and when He prayed. He was surrounded by the same circumstances which touch our lives, and prayer was the mighty weapon which He used repeatedly.

In the four gospel records, there are not less than fifteen recorded occasions on which Christ prayed. From these we may learn lessons that can strengthen us in our own prayer life. We will not examine all fifteen passages in their chronological order, but rather we will attempt to present a composite picture and glean lessons from the whole.

HIS MINISTRY COMMENCED WITH PRAYER

> Now when all the people were baptized, it came to pass, that Jesus also being baptized, and praying (Lk 3:21).

Matthew 3:17 and Mark 1:9-11 both tell of Christ's baptism, but only Luke adds, "and praying." This was the beginning of His public ministry, and He dared not commence it without the anointing of the Holy Spirit. Look again at Luke's account:

> And praying, the heaven was opened, and the Holy Ghost descended in a bodily shape like a dove upon him (Lk 3:21-22).

From this passage, we learn that the occasion of prayer was for Jesus the occasion of power. And we must assume that during those "hidden" years in Nazareth He had developed the habit of prayer. At the age of twelve He could ask, "Wist ye not that I must be about my Father's business?" (Lk 2:49). To be about God's business must of necessity include prayer. When Christ commenced His public ministry, He was simply continuing the practice of prayer which was already His habit from His youth.

His prayer opened heaven, and both the Father and the Holy Spirit responded. The Father's voice was heard saying, "Thou art my beloved Son; in thee I am well pleased," and the Holy Spirit "descended in a bodily shape like a dove upon Him" (Lk 3:22). It was this special anointing, in answer to Christ's prayer, that convinced John that He was the Messiah, the Son of God (Jn 1:32-34).

Dr. G. Campbell Morgan pointed out the fact that the word used in Luke 3:21-22 to express the activity of prayer is *proseuchomai,* which literally means to wish forward or to desire onward. It is the first mention of our Lord praying, and it is most revealing. He is seen in an attitude of devotion, desire, and dependence upon the Father and the Spirit. It was a prayer of faith and confidence. It looked forward to mighty achievements. That is the whole idea in that word *praying.* I would like to see every young candidate called by God into the gospel ministry get started in that way.

In answer to Christ's prayer, the *Father approved* Him,

the *Spirit anointed* Him, and the *people acknowledged* Him. All Christian workers should learn a lesson right here. We dare not depend merely upon our personality, our ability, or our gifts. These all can be used of God, but if we are not men of prayer who depend upon God, we will not have His approval or the Spirit's anointing, nor will our message be effective in the lives of those who hear us.

HIS MINISTRY CONTINUED WITH PRAYER

Mark tells about another occasion on which Christ prayed.

> And in the morning, rising up a great while before day, he went out, and departed into a solitary place, and there prayed. And Simon and they that were with him followed after him. And when they had found him, they said unto him, All men seek for thee. And he said unto them, let us go into the next towns, that I may preach there also: for therefore came I forth (Mk 1:35-38).

The preceding day had been a very busy one for our Lord. He had taught in the synagogue (Mk 1:21-22), cast out demons (Mk 1:23-27), healed Peter's mother-in-law (Mk 1:30-31), and ministered to many who were sick (Mk 1:32-34). He had been pressured by crowds until late, making it an active, long, and exhausting day. We can assume that the following morning He must have needed an extra hour's sleep. But instead, He arose while it was yet dark, slipped away to a quiet place, "and there prayed" (Mk 1:35).

It was in that quiet place of prayer that He received direction for the new day's work. Should He remain in Capernaum, where His efforts were bearing fruit, or should He move on to another town? After He prayed, there was no further question as to the Father's will. Peter wanted Him to stay, for he said to Jesus, "All men seek for thee." But the Lord replied, "Let us go into the next towns, that I may preach there also" (Mk 1:36-38). Prayer had defeated the foe, defined the duties, and directed the path ahead.

We Christians cannot afford to neglect a quiet time alone with God at the beginning of each day. The servant is not greater than his Lord. If our lives and our efforts are to bring forth fruit that will remain, we need divine direction every day. If we make our plans ahead, let them be made only after we have prayed for God's leading. And even then, we must come daily to Him, because He might change our plans. Our sphere of activity for each new day must be preceded by prayer, so as to allow the Holy Spirit to choose for us. Just as our Saviour would not choose His own program without first praying to the Father, neither should we. It is not possible for a Christian to know God's best for him apart from prayer.

His Ministry Counted upon Prayer

Some Christians experience a large measure of success, even to the extent of having fame and honor heaped upon them. No doubt there are those who deserve the commendation they receive. But this sort of thing can present potential dangers. The old, carnal nature, which is ever a part of us, thrives on the plaudits of our fellowmen. We like others to speak well of us, and we readily accept any honors bestowed upon us. However, we do not always know what it is that motivates someone to praise us. In any case, it becomes difficult for any of us to remain humble and dependent upon the Lord when we are being praised by others.

Our Lord faced this very test. Luke says,

> But so much the more went there a fame abroad of him: and great multitudes came together to hear, and to be healed by him of their infirmities. And he withdrew himself into the wilderness, and prayed (Lk 5:15-16).

Jesus had enemies, but He also had many friends and followers—so many that He became famous. Now, note what action He took. He withdrew into the wilderness and prayed. What a lesson there is here for us! I wonder if some of us might not be tempted to count on those many friends who honor and praise us. I imagine it could be quite hard for some of us not to succumb to this temptation. In that crisis, Christ counted on prayer.

When a Christian reaches a new peak of prosperity and prominence, it is time to withdraw himself and pray. Let me warn you that at just such a time we will not feel a great need to pray. We will be tempted to respond to those who speak well of us. But beware! A Christian being used of God can lose his power and usefulness if his heart is lifted up with pride. Prayer meant much to Jesus when fame came to Him; let us also count heavily on prayer in such a crisis.

It is written of King Uzziah of Judah, "As long as he sought the Lord, God made him to prosper" (2 Ch 26:5). But when he reached the peak of prosperity and power, he forgot God, and his heart was lifted up with pride (v.16). He was stricken with leprosy and died a defeated and unwanted man, in loneliness and isolation (vv.21-23). How are the mighty fallen! Beloved Christian, let us never lose our sense of dependence upon God. We must count much on prayer, as did our Lord Jesus Christ. He retreated from the presence and plaudits of men in order to commune with the Father.

His Men Were Chosen in Prayer

It was in the plan and purpose of God that Jesus should choose twelve men who would represent Him after His departure. Luke records the occasion:

> And it came to pass in those days, that he went out into a mountain to pray, and continued all night in prayer to God. And when it was day, he called unto him his disciples: and of them he chose twelve, who also he named apostles (Lk 6:12-13).

There was a particular burden on the Lord's heart that drove Him to that all-night prayer session. The selection of the twelve apostles was an important item of business, calling for prolonged communion with the Father. The

Scripture does not tell us that He had planned to spend that night in prayer, but the immediate circumstances called for prayer.

What were those circumstances? The religious leaders from Judea were stirring up resentment against Him. They dogged His steps and sought to destroy Him. Weary in body and spirit, He resorted to prayer—not one of those brief, quickie prayers we sometimes pray, but a prayer session that lasted the whole night. He knew that His time on earth was not long, and He needed men who could carry on under the same pressures and persecutions He was experiencing. He was arranging for the continuation of His program.

But why an all-night prayer meeting? Could not that selection of men have been made in less time? I know only that some requests are not granted at once. I know also that we tend to choose men on the basis of their outward appearances and personal preferences. Churches have been made to suffer great loss because the leaders did not spend enough time in prayer before calling a pastor. Paul warned Timothy, "Lay hands suddenly on no man" (1 Ti 5:22), and told him not to be guilty of prejudice and partiality (v.21). It is important that God's man be chosen for God's work, and all such choices call for much prayer.

So burdened was our Lord for that solemn task, that He lost all sense of time and prayed on and on until the break of day. And with the new dawn there came the selection of the twelve, some of whom became the penmen of much of the New Testament.

Such waiting upon God was practiced also by some in the early church. Luke writes of the apostles facing the selection of men to carry the gospel to new fields, "As they ministered to the Lord, and fasted, the Holy Ghost said, Separate me Barnabas and Saul for the work whereunto I have called them. And when they had fasted and prayed, and laid their hands on them, they sent them away" (Ac 13:2-3). And that is the way it should be done. Before any church selects a pastor, deacons, or elders, this example in the life of our Lord and of the early church should be given serious consideration.

HIS MIRACLES WERE CONSUMMATED BY PRAYER

The miracles of our Lord have had a strong appeal to the masses of people, both during His lifetime and up to our present day. But not much has been said or written about the relationship of those miracles to His prayer life. In our brief study we will examine two of Christ's miracles — the feeding of the five thousand men plus women and children, and the raising of Lazarus from death and the grave. These two incidents have been selected because they both pertain to the giving and sustaining of life.

Let us look first at the miracle He performed by feeding the multitude. The record of this miracle appears in Matthew, chapter 14; Mark, chapter 6; and John, chapter 6. Matthew and Mark both relate that He prayed before and after the miraculous feeding.

Matthew says there was a "great multitude. . . . about five thousand men, beside women and children" (14:14, 21). The crowds had followed Jesus away from the village to a deserted place; now evening had come, and it was time to eat (14:15). But there was no food to provide for so large a number. The disciples would have dispersed the people, sending them to town, but Jesus said, "They need not depart; give ye them to eat" (14:16). But what would they feed so large a crowd? All three writers say that only five loaves and two fishes were available (Mt 14:17; Mk 6:38; Jn 6:9)—a mere nothing compared to so many people.

Jesus requested the five loaves and the two fishes and commanded the people to be seated on the ground in rows of fifties and hundreds. Then, "He looked up to heaven, and blessed" (Mt 14:19; Mk 6:41). John says, "When he had given thanks" (Jn 6:11).

Go back in your mind and think through the sequence of

events. Jesus knew that His prayer would be answered even before the loaves and fishes were miraculously multiplied. His command to the people to be seated was an act of faith. He fully expected abundant provision of food for all those present. His prayer was one of faith and confidence. "They did all eat and were filled" (Mt 14:20).

> And when he had sent the multitudes away, he went up into a mountain apart to pray: and when the evening was come, he was there alone (Mt 14:23).

That experience in the prayer life of our Lord is deeply instructive. It stands as an example for the prayer life of every child of God. As we meet God's requirements for successful praying, we can ask for our daily bread with the same confidence and assurance that God will supply every need. But be sure you do not miss the grand climax in the story—"He went up into a mountain apart to pray." He had received His request, but the prayer fellowship with His Father continued. Modern Christians grab the handout and say, "So long, God. I'll be back when I need more bread." I prefer to keep in constant touch with the Source of supply, as Jesus did.

We come now to the miracle of giving life to the dead. Only John recorded the miracle of raising Lazarus from death and the grave. Lazarus had been in the tomb four days. A large crowd had gathered, and they were mourning the death of this brother of Mary and Martha. When Jesus arrived at the tomb, He requested that the stone be removed. And then, looking upward, He prayed, "Father, I thank thee that thou hast heard me" (Jn 11:41).

This suggests that before He came to the tomb, He had already prayed about the raising of Lazarus, and the miracle that followed was an answer to that prayer. He was assured of the restoration of Lazarus's life because He was confident that the Father would grant the request. He continued to pray, "And I knew that thou hearest Me always" (Jn 11:42).

There lay the dead body. But Christ believed that God not only *could* but *would* restore life to Lazarus. His prayer was an intercessory one, and the request was granted. We know this because, "he that was dead came forth" (Jn 11:44). As our Lord performed this mightiest of miracles, He linked prayer and praise together. And on this occasion, all who were present were taught some precious lessons about prayer. That was the only reason Christ prayed and thanked the Father in the presence of the crowd standing there. He said,

> And I knew that thou hearest me always: but because of the people which stand by I said it, that they may believe that thou hast sent me (Jn 11:42).

HIS MINISTRY (ON EARTH) CONCLUDED IN PRAYER

Our Lord's last days on earth, just prior to His arrest and trial, were spent in prayer. One of His favorite places to pray was the Garden of Gethsemane. We find the record in Matthew, chapter 26; Mark, chapter 14; and Luke, chapter 22.

Christ turned to His disciples and said, "Sit ye here, while I go and pray yonder" (Mt 26:36). Then taking Peter, James, and John with Him, He entered the garden, and said to them, "My soul is exceeding sorrowful, even unto death" (Mt 26:38). Matthew and Mark tell us He fell on the ground; Luke describes Him in a kneeling position. All three, however, describe the content of His prayer, namely, complete submission to the Father's will. He prayed,

> O my Father, if it be possible, let this cup pass from me: nevertheless not as I will, but as thou wilt (Mt 26:39).

Realizing that within a few hours He would be bearing in His body the full weight and penalty of all the sins of Adam's fallen race, an intense physical and mental struggle began. He commenced to feel a strange, desolate loneliness, an awareness of the coming total isolation. Men were already plotting His death, and soon the Father would black out the sky from His view. He was facing the most crucial experience of His earthly life—one He would escape if it were possible. He realized that the hour had come when He would be made the sin offering for us, and He would experience the awful loneliness of that separation from the Father. But He faced it triumphantly in prayer, in total submission to the divine will.

> He went away again the second time, and prayed, saying, O my Father, if this cup may not pass away from me, except I drink it, thy will be done (Mt 26:42).

When Christ arose from that season of prayer, a great victory had been won. The crisis past, the conquest was complete. He was ready for the cross. Prayer had played an important role in that victory.

We, too, can face life's bitter experiences in the will of God by surrendering our will in prayer. "The cup which my Father hath given me, shall I not drink it?" (Jn 18:11).

We move on to Calvary and those last moments before Christ's death on the cross. His first words in those dying moments were in the form of a prayer in behalf of those very men who had driven the nails through His hands and feet. He prayed, "Father, forgive them; for they know not what they do" (Lk 23:34).

Here is the classic example of an uncommon form of intercessory prayer. It is much easier to pray for ourselves, our loved ones, and our close friends than it is to pray for our enemies. But here we see our Lord at His best, praying for His enemies, who were putting Him to death. He was practicing what He had taught His followers in the Sermon on the Mount:

> Love your enemies, bless them that curse you, do good to them that hate you, and pray for them which despitefully use you, and persecute you (Mt 5:44).

And then His work on earth was complete. Having suffered for the sins of man, He breathed His last breath in a quiet prayer in behalf of those for whom He was dying. And as He yielded up His life, He said, "Father, into thy hands I commend my spirit" (Lk 23:46).

This was His final prayer on earth. It was a prayer of confidence. I can think of no better way for a person to die than in sweet communion with God.

His Ministry (in Heaven) Continues in Prayer

When our Lord left earth and ascended to the Father, He did not cease to pray. He still prays.

> Wherefore he is able also to save them to the uttermost that come unto God by him, seeing he ever liveth to make intercession for them (Heb 7:25).

Christ is a "priest for ever" (Heb 7:17), and He "continueth ever," having "an unchangeable priesthood" (Heb 7:24). Therefore there is never a single moment when His prayers in our behalf do not reach our heavenly Father. He exercises the priestly function of His office without interruption or interference, so that all who are His can never be lost. He is able to save completely. He saved us by His propitiatory work in His death; He keeps us saved through His priestly work in heaven. The fruit of His propitiatory work is our salvation; the fruit of His priestly work is our security. In the performance of His priestly ministry, He does not live for Himself, but for all who have come to God through Him. He prays for our sake. That is what He is doing in heaven now.

Christ is our "great high priest" (Heb 4:14), yes, the greatest of high priests, whose prayers abound with the power of deity. No one ever prayed for us who is as glorious as our High Priest. His prayers are superior to the prayers of all the saints. Because He lives continuously, He intercedes continuously. The Christian gospel embraces the living Priest as well as the dying Saviour. Christ reconciled us to

God by His death (Ro 5:10), and He represents us before God in His life, "now to appear in the presence of God for us" (Heb 9:24). As Christ entreated the Father in behalf of Peter (Lk 22:31-32), so He intercedes at this very moment in our behalf. His present ministry of intercession and intervention is just as real and vital now as was His death on the cross for our sins. We are ever dependent upon our eternal Priest and His continuing prayers for us.

16

Questions and Answers

1. Can a person be saved without praying for salvation?

I will not attempt to answer this question with a yes or no. I will begin by affirming my belief that salvation is a free and full pardon offered by grace to the worst of sinners, and not dependent upon works (Eph 2:8-9; Titus 3:5).

However, I have not been able to see how a sinner can receive salvation without wanting it and asking for it. I do not believe that anyone will be saved merely by saying prayers, nor do I believe that without prayer anyone will be saved.

I have stood beside many dying persons, some of whom were not saved. Never have I given up hope that any person can be saved on a deathbed. But I will not offer false hope to a person, even on his deathbed, if that one does not want salvation enough to ask God for it. Prayer is not the only prerequisite for salvation, but it does seem to be a necessary one. "For whosoever shall call upon the name of the Lord shall be saved" (Ro 10:13).

2. Why is it the common practice to bow the head when praying?

To the best of my knowledge, the Bible does not answer this question. However, there are numerous examples of this practice recorded in the Scriptures: "And the man bowed his head, and worshipped the LORD" (Gen. 24:26; see also Ex

4:31; 12:27; 2 Ch 29:30). Bowing the head is not the only posture in prayer, but it is one of those mentioned in the Bible. The act itself suggests reverence and respect. Subjects bow to their Sovereign.

But there is also some practical value in bowing the head when we pray. Usually we also close our eyes, and this enables us to shut out anything that might prevent us from concentrating on the Lord. Anything can be considered beneficial if it reduces disturbances and distractions when we are praying.

3. Does God always answer the Christian's prayer?

Yes! I do not believe that there has ever been an unanswered prayer. The answer will come in one of several different ways. First, there is the *direct* answer, when we pray for a specific request, and it is granted at once, without delay. It is a thrilling experience to see God respond instantly in granting the thing for which we asked.

Second, there is the *delayed* answer. The request is granted, but it is deferred. The postponement is intentional on God's part. The need is real, and the request is valid, but our timing is off. A request deferred is not a request denied. God knows best when to give the thing for which we have prayed. We should not become discouraged if our request is not granted at once. Let God work in His own time. His timing is always perfect. After you have prayed about a matter, leave it with Him. God's clock is never slow.

Moses prayed and asked God to permit him to enter the promised land. The answer was delayed 1500 years. Moses did not get there until Jesus brought him there on the mount of transfiguration.

Third, there is the *different* answer. Because of our selfishness and shortsightedness, we are not always aware of exactly what we need. "We know not what we should pray for as we ought" (Ro 8:26). The apostle Paul thought his need was the healing of his thorn in the flesh, but that was *not* his need at all. After he had prayed earnestly three times for healing, he had to be shown by God that he was not asking for the right thing. Paul thought he needed healing, but God knew Paul needed His grace (2 Co 12:7-9). In this instance, prayer did not change the situation about which Paul had prayed, but prayer did change Paul. A different answer, of God's choosing, is always best.

Fourth, there is the *denial*. I doubt that there are many Christians who have an understanding, much less an appreciation, of this kind of an answer to prayer. The average Christian who does not have his requests granted will complain that God did not answer his prayer. Such a conclusion is wrong. When God says no, that is an answer. Elijah prayed that he would die, but his foolish request was denied (1 Ki 19:4). I have thanked God on several occasions that He did not grant me some of my desires.

4. Is it important that Christians pray audibly?

There are advantages in praying audibly. Personally, I get a feeling of talking to a real, living Person when I pray aloud. The psalmist said, "I cried unto God with my voice, even unto God with my voice; and he gave ear unto me (Ps 77:1). If we pray audibly in the privacy of our room, it will help us when we are asked to pray in public. When we use our voice, we are better able to concentrate and to control our words.

However, prayer need not be audible to be heard by God. I have done some of my own praying silently while traveling in a plane or automobile, or when sitting in a public meeting. Very often, the thought of some person is a call to pray for that person, and that thought might come to mind at any time or place. Not every situation will be conducive to giving voice to our petitions.

5. Can Satan hinder our prayers?

There is little doubt about Satan being able to hinder the prayers of God's children. Satan works through his many demons. In the New Testament, the demons are called "unclean spirits" (Mt 12:43; Mk 1:23-27) and "seducing spirits" (1 Ti 4:1). These evil spirits can and do attack the bodies of human beings. They have been known to paralyze one's voice (Mt 9:32-33); smite with blindness (Mt 12:22); torment both mind and body to induce a suicidal tendency (Mk 9:17-29); and cause a disease to attack one's body (Lk 13:11-17; 2 Co 12:7).

Prayer is work, and we do our best work when body and mind are sound. I believe prayer is the Christian exercise which the devil works hardest to hinder. Someone has said, "The devil trembles when he sees the weakest saint upon his knees."

I can recall having restless nights when it was difficult for me to sleep. I would decide to use those waking moments to pray, but I would not be praying long before I would become drowsy and fall asleep. The devil does not care if I lose sleep, but he does care if I pray. "Be sober, be vigilant; because your adversary the devil, as a roaring lion, walketh about, seeking whom he may devour" (1 Pe 5:8). "Be ye therefore sober, and watch unto prayer" (1 Pe 4:7).

6. Does prayer change things?

Yes and no! There are times when prayer does change things. On the other hand, prayer more frequently changes the person who prays.

In the case of Hezekiah, prayer changed things. God told Hezekiah that his time had come to die. Hezekiah prayed that God would extend his life, and in response to that prayer God gave His child fifteen years more to live (2 Ki 20:1-11). God did not necessarily change His will, but He did will a change.

In Paul's experience, prayer did not change things, but it did change the man. Paul prayed three times for bodily healing. God did not heal Paul; his physical condition remained unchanged. However, Paul's attitude toward his "thorn" and toward God changed when he discovered the sufficiency of God's grace (2 Co 12:7-9).

Man is basically selfish; therefore his prayer requests are sometimes selfish. We expect God to change His plans for our benefit. However, if we pray for God's will in our lives, He might not change our circumstances, but He will, through prayer, change our attitude toward Him and toward our circumstances. We cannot change the mind of God and get Him to do that which is not His plan and purpose. That is not the purpose of prayer. We are dealing with a moral God of truth, righteousness, and holiness; these attributes He cannot change.

Do not be carried away by the motto which says, "Prayer changes things." God knows when something should be changed, and He knows when our hearts need changing. When a problem arises, take it to God in prayer, following the formula in Philippians 4:6-7, which says, "Be careful for nothing; but in every thing by prayer and supplication with thanksgiving let your requests be made known unto God. And the peace of God, which passeth all understanding, shall keep your hearts and minds through Christ Jesus."

Do not worry about anything, but pray about everything. And be certain your prayer is "with thanksgiving," which means thanking God in advance, whatever the outcome. After you have prayed about the matter, the problem will still be very real, but your heart attitude will be changed. Worry will give way to peace.

7. Is it ever proper to address a prayer directly to the Holy Spirit?

Most prayers in the Bible are addressed to God the Father. Jesus said, "After this manner therefore pray ye: Our Father which art in heaven" (Mt 6:9). "Whatsoever ye shall ask the Father in my name, he will give it you" (Jn 16:23). To these statements Paul added, "For this cause I bow my knees unto the Father of our Lord Jesus Christ" (Eph 3:14). From these and many other passages, it seems that believers usually call God "Father" in their prayers. Jesus also called Him "Father" when He prayed (Jn 17:1,5,11,21,24,25).

On the other hand, I cannot find anything in the Bible to prohibit a believer's praying to Christ or to the Holy Spirit. Each member of the Trinity performs a unique ministry. Stephen prayed to the Lord Jesus (Ac 7:59). It is a perfectly natural and normal thing for any Christian to thank Jesus for dying for his sins. I have done this frequently in my own prayers. And why not? It was not the first nor the third Person in the Trinity who died on the cross. When I thank Jesus for shedding His blood for me, I address Him personally and directly.

It is the function of the Holy Spirit to teach the Christian (Jn 14:26; 16:13; 1 Co 2:9-11). When I come to study the Bible, I ask the Holy Spirit to guide and teach me. I do not ask the Father or Jesus to do that for me which is the prescribed ministry of the Holy Spirit. For many years I have prayed in this way to the Holy Spirit, and the requests have been granted. I cannot conceive of God refusing to answer such a prayer. The members of the Godhead are coequal; each can be addressed in prayer.

8. Why pray at all?

There are those persons who believe that inasmuch as God has blessed all believers "with all spiritual blessings in heavenly places in Christ" (Eph 1:3), there is no need for Christians to ask any request of God. To this kind of false reasoning there is a scriptural refutation.

The Lord Jesus said, "Men ought always to pray, and not to faint" (Lk 18:1). Added to this exhortation is the command of the Holy Spirit through Paul to pray about "every thing" (Phil 4:6), and to "pray without ceasing" (1 Th 5:17). There are many Scriptures that encourage Christians to pray about everything which touches their daily lives (Eph 6:18; 2 Th 3:1-2; 1 Ti 2:1-4). Why pray at all? The answer to this question is simple: we pray because God's Word commands us to pray. Since it is true that "Ye have not, because ye ask not" (Ja 4:2), then we ought to heed those commands in the Bible that tell us to pray.

9. What did Jesus mean by *importunity* in the prayer in Luke 11:8?

This is the only appearance of the word *importunity* in the Bible. In the context, it suggests the idea of earnestness and perseverance in prayer. In other words, Jesus taught that we are not to feel ashamed about persisting in our asking. An Old Testament example of importunate prayer is Abraham's praying in behalf of the righteous souls in Sodom (Gen 18:23-33). In the New Testament, the Syro-Phoenician woman's prayer in behalf of her daughter is an illustration of importunity in prayer (Mt 15:22-28).

In His parable of the persistent friend, Jesus taught that if persistence can obtain help from a neighbor, then most assuredly, earnest prayer will get response from our heavenly Father.

10. How can I learn to pray?

First, bear with me as I quote a statement made by Thomas Edison in 1921. He said, "We don't know the millionth part of one percent about anything. We don't know what water is. We don't know what light is. We don't know what gravitation is. We don't know what electricity is. We don't know what heat is. We have a lot of hypotheses about these things, but that is all. But we do not let our ignorance about all these things deprive us of their use."

I am certain that there is much about prayer that we will never learn in this life. However, we must take that knowledge which available in the Bible and start using it. We learn by doing.

In this little book, you have just read some guidelines for

praying. Now, get alone with God, and speak to Him in honesty and simplicity.

> Prayer is the simplest form of speech
>   That infant lips can try;
> Prayer the sublimest strains that reach
>   The Majesty on High.

JAMES MONTGOMERY